Oxford Stage Company & Dumbfounded Theatre
present

T0316250

ROSE BERND

By **Gerhart Hauptmann**
In a new version by **Dennis Kelly**

Directed by **Gari Jones**
Design by **Jon Bausor**
Lighting by **Tim Mascall**
Sound by **Adrienne Quartly**

First performance of this production as part of **The Last Waltz Season**
on 22 March 2005 at the Arcola Theatre, London.

The Last Waltz Season also features *Musik* by Frank Wedekind,
translated and adapted by Neil Fleming, and *Professor Bernhardi* by
Arthur Schnitzler in a new version by Samuel Adamson.

austrian cultural forum^{lon}

Oxford Stage Company is supported by

Oxford Stage Company and Dumbfounded Theatre present

ROSE BERND

by **Gerhart Hauptmann**

Cast

Flamm	John Dougall
Rose Bernd	Caroline Hayes
Streckmann	John Lloyd Fillingham
Marthel	Cydney Folan
Old Bernd	Fred Pearson
August	Roger Evans
Mrs Flamm	Yvonne Gidden
Hahn	Jake Harders
Heinzel	Tom Godwin
Kleinart	Dale Rapley
Golisch	Bertie Carvel
Mrs Golisch	Lucy Briers
Constable	Bertie Carvel

The cast of *Rose Bernd* is drawn from an ensemble of actors which also includes: Mariah Gale, Christopher Godwin, John Stahl and Deka Walmsley.

Creative Team

Adaptor	Dennis Kelly
Director	Gari Jones
Designer	Jon Bausor
Lighting Designer	Tim Mascall
Sound Designer	Adrienne Quartly
Season Lighting Designers	Tim Mascall & Neil Sloan
Literal translator	Anthony Meech
Costume Supervisor	Sallyann Dicksee
Fight Director	Kieran Bew
Assistant Director	Eleanor Green
Assistant Designers	Anna Jones
	Tom Rogers
Production Manager	Chris Umney
Stage Managers	Laura Farrell
	Nicholas Green
Assistant Stage Managers	Sarah Grange
	Ciara Fanning
Production Electrician	Jenny Abbott
Production Photographer	Alessandro Evangelista
Graphic Design	Pansy Aung & Winnie Wong
Season Producers	Mark Rosenblatt
	Neil Laidlaw

Production Acknowledgements

Petra Tauscher, Conrad Lynch, Sibylle Wunderlich, Gemma Hancock, Anne McNulty, Anneliese Davidsen, the Young Vic, Linzie Hunter at Mountview Academy, Paul Anderson at Sparks Theatrical Hire, the staff of the British Library, the London Library and the Goethe Institute.

Special thanks to

Sir Tom Stoppard, Peter Skrine, David Lan, Patricia Benecke, Claire Frewin, The Wellcome Trust, Austrian Cultural Forum, Mercers' Charitable Foundation, Caird Company and the Academy of Young Jewish Artists.

Writer's note

I want to say right away that I don't speak any German except to say 'a beer, please' and 'sorry, I don't speak any German'. The way this process worked was that Tony Meech did a literal translation which I then worked from. There is a fair amount of controversy surrounding this way of doing things but once we accept it, we can then accept that what we are going to make is an entirely new work based on the original (and there is a good argument to say that this is what happens when any translation is attempted). The process then becomes about taking decisions.

When approaching the translation I didn't want to find an English rural equivalent of Silesia in the late nineteenth century, partly because I felt that there wasn't one and partly because I've never lived in the country so I wouldn't know one if it kicked me up the arse. Though *Rose Bernd* wasn't exactly written in a dialect, much of it was cut down and shortened from 'high German' and it has the flavour of an accent, something that was quite revolutionary at the time. So I trimmed the text where possible and removed as many pronouns as I could from the poorer characters, particularly when it referred to themselves, perhaps dehumanising them in this claustrophobic, God-crammed society. So instead of saying 'I want' or 'I don't' they just say 'want' or 'don't' giving a more general selfless feel to their lives. The exception to this is often Streckmann, a dangerous rebel who wants things for himself.

We have also become used to drama that is very 'actioned'; we ask that lines do something rather than explain something. I have applied this principle to this play as much as possible. This has meant occasionally manipulating the text to suit my own purposes instead of Hauptmann's, but he's been dead for so long that I thought he wouldn't mind.

I apologise to anyone who knows the play in German and whose favourite bits I have cut out, but those people can always read them in the original text where they're still there.

Dennis Kelly, 2005
Writer

Rose Bernd

Last year I spent a little too much time in the British Library. My mission was to find 3 rarely (if ever) seen plays by great German writers from around the turn of the 20th century. I'm a big fan of the equivalent period of British theatre (George Bernard Shaw, Granville Barker, Galsworthy, DH Lawrence) and, having German grandparents, I was curious to know what German theatre was up to before Brecht burst on to the scene and eclipsed virtually everybody. I found a wealth of plays, some awful, some ok and a handful of gems. A number of which were written by Gerhart Hauptmann, by far the least famous playwright in our season. Yet, way back then, he was the man. Inheritor of Goethe's mantle, Nobel Prize winner, translated across Europe and an out-and-out living German legend. In fact, if you go to the British Library you'll find a 10-volume, English-language collection of Hauptmann's genre-defying plays translated before 1914.

This is where I found *Rose Bernd*. The translator had seen fit to turn 1900 Silesian peasants into 'ooh-aar' Somerset farmers. But beneath this distracting relocation lay a simple, passionate tragedy.

Hauptmann was an innovator. Chekhov credits Hauptmann's *Lonely Lives* as an inspiration for his three masterpieces. Hauptmann himself berated Strindberg for stealing the psycho-surreal innovations of his play *Hannele* and turning them into *A Dream Play*. In *Rose Bernd* he's up to the same old tricks. Inspired by an actual court case in which he was foreman of the jury, Hauptmann shows working-class people to be as complex, flawed and passionate as the dickey-bowed Berliner audiences watching the play.

Dennis Kelly's translation is exceptional. I asked him to do it after reading his startling play *Debris* and spending a wonderful afternoon at the Cottesloe watching a semi-staged reading of his translation of Peter Karpati's *The Fourth Gate*. In his own work, Dennis creates very odd worlds but allows his characters, however unstable or deranged, to speak with a conviction in their own perspectives. Which seemed perfect for the strange, god-fearing rural backwaters of *Rose Bernd*.

This is *Rose Bernd*'s first appearance in London. I hope you enjoy it.

Mark Rosenblatt, 2005
Artistic Director
Dumbfounded Theatre

Cast in alphabetical order

LUCY BRIERS Mrs Golisch

Training: Bristol Old Vic Theatre School.
Theatre: Credits include Miss Shotgraven in *The Solid Gold Cadillac* (West End); Edward/Betty in *Cloud Nine* (Crucible, Sheffield) for which she received a TMA Nomination for Best Supporting Actress in 2004; Electra in *Electra* (Gate, London); Laura in *Teeth 'N Smiles* (Crucible, Sheffield); Charlotte in *Don Juan* (Crucible, Sheffield); Desdemona in *Othello* and Ginnie in *Outside Edge* (New Vic Theatre); Maggie in *Keepers* (Hampstead Theatre); Paulina in *The Winter's Tale* (Southwark Playhouse); Phebe in *As You Like It* (Crucible, Sheffield and Lyric, Hammersmith); Verity King in *Spike* (Nuffield, Southhampton); and Rosaura in *The Venetian Twins* (Oxford Stage Company).
TV: Credits include *Wives And Daughters*, *Dangerfield* and Mary Bennett in *Pride and Prejudice* (BBC); *Poirot: The Hollow* (Granada); *Prince William* (ABC); *Bodies, Shadow Play*, *The Bill*, *Beast,* and *Imogen's Face* (ITV).
Film: *Perks* (Finalist in LA Short Film Festival, 2003).
Radio: Credits include *The Woman In Black, Mary, Mary, Between The Ears, Daughters of Britannia, Henry IV Parts I & II,* and *Last of the Barsetshire Chronicles*, all for BBC Radio Drama.

BERTIE CARVEL Golisch / Constable

Training: RADA
Theatre: Credits include the title role in *Macbeth* (en masse for Union Theatre); *Victory?* (Donmar Theatre); and *Revelations* (Hampstead Theatre).
TV and Film: Credits include *The Genius of Beethoven* (BBC); *Bombshell* (Shed Productions for ITV); *Agatha Christie: A Life in Pictures* (Wall to Wall for BBC); *The Lost World of Mitchell and Kenyon* (BBC); *Suits and Swipes* (New York Film Academy) and *Hawking* (BBC).
Radio: Bertie has also recorded over 30 radio plays for the BBC, including *Trilby, Diary of a Nobody, The Odyssey, The Pallisers, Kamikaze, Portugal, D Day,* and *The Entertainer*.

JOHN DOUGALL Flamm

Training: Royal Scottish Academy of Music and Drama.

Theatre: Work for the Royal Shakespeare Company includes: *Hamlet, Love in a Wood, Macbeth* (Stratford / London / Japan / US), *Measure for Measure, The Two Gentlemen of Verona, The Merchant of Venice, The Cherry Orchard, Faust, The Devil is an Ass, Peter Pan, The Winters Tale, The Crucible* (UK / Poland). Work for the English Shakespeare Company includes: *The Henrys, The War of the Roses, Richard II, Richard III, The Winters Tale, Coriolanus,* and *Romeo and Juliet* (Old Vic, West End, national and international tours). Theatre credits in London include: *The Shadow of a Gunman, John Bull's Other Island* (Tricycle), *Measure for Measure* (Globe); *Americans, The Cherry Orchard* (Oxford Stage Company); *Another Country* (Queens Theatre); *The Cherry Orchard* (Aldwych); *St Joan* (Strand); *Dr Faustus* (Greenwich Theatre); and *Twelfth Night, Macbeth* and *King Lear* (St George's Theatre). Other theatre includes: *Present Laughter* (Theatre Royal Bath / tour); *Arcadia* (Northampton / Salisbury); *Hay Fever* (Oxford Stage Company); *Romeo and Juliet* (Nottingham); *Of Mice and Men* (Birmingham); *Tess of the D'Urbervilles* (Edinburgh Festival); *The Comedy of Errors, Translations, Peter Pan* (Lyric, Belfast); *Lysistrata, Treasure Island* (Worcester); and *The Lass wi' the Muckle Mou* (Pitlochry).

TV: Credits include *The Houseman's Tale, Dunrulin', As Time Goes By, Taggart, The Bill, The Negotiator, Monarch of the Glen, Macbeth, Randall and Hopkirk (Deceased), He Knew He Was Right* and *Measure for Measure.*

ROGER EVANS August

Theatre: Credits include *Woyzeck* (The Gate); *How Love is Spelt* (Bush Theatre); *The King Stag* (Young Vic Theatre); *Art and Guff* (Soho Theatre/ Sgript Cymru); *Everything Must Go* (Sherman Theatre); *Gas Station Angel* (Royal Court International tour); and *Scum & Civility* and *The Man Who Never Yet Saw Woman's Nakedness* (Royal Court International Festival).

TV: *Casualty, Doctors, The Bill, Murphy's Law, Absolute Power, Nuts and Bolts, The Bench, Bradford In My Dreams, Sleeping With The TV On, A Mind to Kill, Rhinoceros, Crime Traveller,* and *Wonderful You.*

Film: *All or Nothing, Human Traffic,* and *Suckerfish.*

JOHN LLOYD FILLINGHAM Streckmann

Training: Welsh College of Music and Drama.
Theatre: Credits include *Abigail's Party* (The
Duke's, Lancaster); *Titus Andronicus, Measure
for Measure, A Midsummer Night's Dream* and
The Taming of the Shrew (all for the RSC); *The
Birthday Party* (Crucible Theatre, Sheffield); *In
Celebration* (Chichester Festival Theatre); *The
Contractor* and *Making Noise Quietly* (Oxford
Stage Company and West End); *Sleeping Around*
(Paines Plough); *The Tempest, The Glass
Menagerie, The Rise and Fall of Little Voice* (including national tour), *A
Christmas Carol* (Bristol Old Vic); *The Glory of the Garden* (Duke of
York's, London); *Road* and *The Doctor's Dilemma* (Royal Exchange,
Manchester); *The Importance of Being Earnest, Spring and Port Wine*
and *Waiting for Godot* (Octagon Theatre, Bolton); *The Comedy of Errors*
and *The Tempest* (Nottingham Playhouse and international tour); *The
Atheist's Tragedy* (Birmingham Repertory Theatre); *Amadeus* (Gateway,
Chester); and *I Do* (National Theatre Studio).
TV: Credits include *Foyle's War, Casualty, Walter, My Secret Life, The
Last Romantics, The Vice, A + E, Coronation Street, Cold Feet,
September Song, Children's Ward, The Royal, Crocodile Shoes, The
Bill, Spatz,* and *B & B.*
Radio: *The Ghost of Federico Garcia Lorca, Henry IV Parts I and II* and
School for Scandal for BBC Radio 3; and *Healthy Pursuits, Cozzy's
Last Stand, Letters of Introduction, Looking for Alice, Gabriella and The
Gargoyles, Lost Empires, A Stone's Throw from the Sea, Stolen Kisses,*
and *Pino Pelosi* for BBC Radio 4.

CYDNEY FOLAN Marthel

Cydney is studying for her A Levels at Bishop
Challoner Sixth Form College. In her spare time
she works Front of House at the Half Moon
Theatre. She is currently directing a devised
production for her college.

YVONNE GIDDEN Mrs Flamm

Training: Central School of Speech and Drama.
Theatre: Credits include *The Crucible* (Ipswich); *Irma La Douce* (Shaftesbury Theatre); *The Wizz* and *Strange Fruit* (Sheffield Crucible); *Measure for Measure* (National Theatre / Mexico Festival); *Here There is Darkness* (Lyric Theatre, Hammersmith); *The Cat and the Canary* (Farnham Redgrace); *Young Writers Festival* (Royal Court); *Strange Fruit* (Liverpool); *Little Shop of Horrors* (Tour of Australia); *Carmen Jones* (Sheffield Crucible); *Animal Farm* and *Pied Piper* (National Theatre); *Romeo and Juliet* (Temba Theatre); *Wind in the Willows* (Birmingham Rep); *Black and White Minstrels* (Kings Head); *Alma* (This is Now Theatre Co, for which she was nominated Time Out Best Actress Award); *Trickle Down Town* (Calypso Productions); and *Generations of the Dead* (Contact Theatre, Manchester). Yvonne participated in the reading of *Island Wedding* (Talawa Theatre Company) and played Bernice in *Member of The Wedding* (Wimbledon Studio Theatre). Most recently she played various parts in *Bites* (Mama Quillo at The Bush Theatre).
TV: *Walcott, Take the Stage, Take a Nice Girl Like You, The Brief, Domestic Bliss, We'll Think of Something, The Growing Pains of Adrian Mole, Split Screen, Casualty, South of the Border, The Manageress, Paper Mask, Desmonds, Inspector Morse, London's Burning* and Edwina in four episodes of *Big Bad World.* She recently filmed Mrs Obugali in *Think Murder* (Freemantle) and Welfare Officer in *Passer By* (BBC).
Film: Doctor in Kenneth Branagh's *Hamlet.*

TOM GODWIN Heinzel

Training: Ecole Jacques Lecoq.
Theatre: Credits include *Volpone* (Royal Exchange, Manchester); *Skylight* (Vaudeville); *Elizabeth Rex* (Birmingham Rep); *Secret Heart* (Manchester Royal Exchange); *For One Night Only* (Clod Ensemble at BAC); *Robin Hood* (Chipping Norton); *King Lear* (St Marthe, Paris); *The Fantastic Flaw* (Park Avenue Productions, Tokyo); *One* (Jamworks at Truman Brewery); *Signals of Distress* (The Flying Machine at Soho Rep, New York); *Gigantones* (Porto 2001 and international tour); and *DriveRideWalk* (Bridewell).
For Blow Up Theatre Company: *Somebody To Love* (international tour) and *The Illusion Brothers* (Total Theatre award winner 2003, Edinburgh Festival).

TV: Credits include *Waking the Dead, Grease Monkeys, Eastenders, My Dad's The Prime Minister, Anchor Me, Battleplan,* and *Sword of Honour.*
Film: *The Mourners.*

JAKE HARDERS Hahn

Training: Grotowski Center, Poland; Central School of Speech and Drama.
Theatre: Credits include *Candida* (Oxford Stage Company) – nominated for 2005 Ian Charleson Award.
TV: *The Genius of Beethoven* and *Foyle's War.*

CAROLINE HAYES Rose Bernd

Theatre: Credits include *The Real Thing* (Donmar Warehouse); *The Crucible* (Hope Theatre); *Crazyface* (Bristol Old Vic); and *Our Country's Good* (HTV Studio).
TV: Credits include *Inspector Lynley, Perfectly Frank, Servants, First Degree, Casualty, Down To Earth, Doctors, Star Hunter, The Bill, As If, The Sins, Safe as Houses, The Scarlet Pimpernel, The Tenth Kingdom, Wing and A Prayer,* and *Wavelength.*
Film: Credits include *Maybe Baby.*
Radio: Credits include *Magpie Stories* and *The Sound of Silence.*

FRED PEARSON Old Bernd

Theatre: Credits include *Woyzeck* (The Gate); *Serjeant Musgrave's Dance* (Oxford Stage Company); *The Prince of Homburg* (RSC/Lyric Hammersmith); *John Gabriel Borkman* (ETT and national tour); and *After the Gods* (Hampstead Theatre).
Fred has worked extensively for the National Theatre, the Royal Shakespeare Company, the Royal Court, and Joint Stock.
TV: Credits include *The Great Ship, Midsomer Murders, Hear the Silence, State of Play, As Time Goes By,* and *A&E.*
Film: *My Name is Modesty, Priest,* and *American Friends.*

DALE RAPLEY Kleinart

Training: Bristol Old Vic Theatre School.
Theatre: Credits include Bill in *Mamma Mia* (Prince Edward & Prince of Wales); Dexter in *High Society*; Oberon in *A Midsummer Night's Dream* (Regent's Park); Arnold Champion Cheney in *The Circle* (Oxford Stage Co/National tour); Snug in *A Midsummer Night's Dream* (RSC); Bluntschli in *Arms and the Man*; Charles Appelby in *Eden End* (West Yorkshire Playhouse); Leading Actor in *Six Characters* (Young Vic); Elyot in *Private Lives*, Lec in *Virtual Reality*; Valder in *A Word From Our Sponsor*; Robert in *Dreams from a Summer House*; A in *Village Wooing*; Frenchy in *Rocket to the Moon* (Stephen Joseph Theatre); The Doctor in *The Ignoramus and the Maniac* (White Bear Theatre); Peter in *Company* (Library Theatre, Manchester); Bob Cratchit in *A Christmas Carol*; Mr. Tebrick in *Lady Into Fox* (Lyric Hammersmith); Harry in *Flora the Red Menace*; Axel in *Playing with Fire* (Orange Tree Theatre); Cliff in *Cabaret* (Derby Playhouse); Jake and Mead in *Safe Sex* (Contact Theatre); Jack in *The Importance of Being Earnest* (Belgrade Theatre, Coventry); Bill Paradene in *Good Morning Bill* (Watermill Theatre, Newbury); Walker in *Prin*; Paul Bratter in *Barefoot in the Park* (Wolsey Theatre, Ipswich); Bassanio in *The Merchant of Venice* (Ludlow/Holland Park); Greek Chorus in *Philoctetes*; Sebastian in *The Tempest* (Cheek By Jowl); Dick Tassel in *The Happiest Days of Your Life*; Mortimer in *Mary Stuart*; Hastings in *She Stoops to Conquer*; Gerald in *When We Are Married* (Salisbury Playhouse); Angelo and Others in *Piaf*; Banquo in *Macbeth*; John in *The Hired Man* (Royal Northampton); Clark in *Arturo Ui*; Ferdinand in *The Tempest*; The Mad Hatter in *Alice*; Valere in *Tartuffe;* and Edward in *Blood Brothers* (Swan Theatre, Worcester).
Television: Credits include *Poirot, Doctors, Spooks, Silent Witness, Aquila II, Eastenders, Casualty, Julia Jekyll and Harriet Hyde, The Peter Townsend Story, Between the Lines, The Vision Thing, Medics,* and *Birds of a Feather.*
Film: Credits include *Paper Mask.*
Radio: Credits include *The Forsyte Chronicles*, *The Beaux Stratagems*, *Mother Courage*, *Three Sisters*, *The Vicissitudes of Evangeline,* and *Laughter in the Dark.*

Writer

GERHART HAUPTMANN

Born in Poland in 1892 the young Hauptmann studied sculpture in Brenslow before turning to writing. Heavily influenced by the playwright Henrik Ibsen's realist works he began experimenting with various literary ideas and forms, settling on drama as his preferred medium. His first play *Var Sonnenaufgang* (1889, *Before Dawn*, 1909) is a prime example of German naturalistic drama and traces the disintegration in human morals when a peasant family discover sudden wealth.

Many of his plays use the peasant class as their protagonist, which was unusual for the period in which Hauptmann was writing, as opposed to focusing on the individual or bourgeois class. This technique is most famous in works such as *Die Weber* (1892, *trans*. 1899), a drama of social protest about a group of Silesian weavers. In later plays Hauptmann disregarded this naturalistic technique in favour of a far more romanticised and symbolic verse form, found in plays such as *Die Verinkene Gloke* (1896, *The Sunken Bell*, 1898), a fantasy about a struggling artist. In plays such as *Rose Bernd* (1903, *trans*. 1913) and *Furmann Henshal* (1898, *trans*. 1913) he explores the plights of the individual who is destroyed by his or her own moral shortcomings and the tragedy this causes.

Also known for his epic poems and novels, Hauptmann was awarded the Nobel Prize for literature in 1912. He died in 1946 in Agentendorg.

Creative Team

DENNIS KELLY Adaptor

Dennis studied Drama and Theatre Arts at Goldsmiths College. His plays are *Debris* (Latchmere 2003, BAC, Traverse Studio and the Burgtheatre, Vienna 2004); *Blackout* (WCMD & Soho Theatre Festival 2003); *The Colony* (The Wire, Radio Three), which has just won Best European Radio Drama at the Prix Europa and Best Script at the Radio and Music Awards; *The Fourth Gate*, a translation of a play by Peter Karparti for the National Theatre Studio. He has also written for BBC 3's *Monkey Dust*.

Current work includes *Osama the Hero* for the Hampstead Theatre (May 2005), *After the End* for Paines Plough (August 2005) and *12 Shares*, a play for BBC Radio 4 (October 2005), as well as planned productions of *Debris* in Italy, Germany and Holland in 2005. Dennis is associate playwright with Paines Plough.

GARI JONES Director

Gari's directing credits include *Speak Truth To Power* (West End), *Look Europe* (Almeida), *Dearest Daddy, Darling Daughter* (Young Vic), *Monologue* (Almeida at the National Theatre and Lincoln Center, New York), *Pinter Sketches* (National Theatre), *The Caretaker* (English Touring Theatre and National Theatre), and *Biloxi Blues* (Jerwood Vanburgh). As writer/ director Gari's work has toured Europe and played at the Edinburgh Festival.

JON BAUSOR Designer

Jon read Music as a choral scholar at Oxford University and studied at Exeter College of Art before training on the Motley Theatre Design Course. He was a finalist in the Linbury Prize for Stage Design 2000. Recent theatre designs include *Frankenstein* (Derby Playhouse); *Bread and Butter* (Tricycle Theatre); *Sanctuary The Tempest* (National Theatre); *Winners, Interior, The Exception and the Rule, The New Tenant, The Soul of Chien-Nu Leaves her Body* (Young Vic); *The Taming of the Shrew* (Theatre Royal Plymouth / Thelma Holt Ltd); *Tartuffe, Ghosts in the Cottonwoods* (Arcola); *The America Play* (RADA); *Switchback, Possible Worlds* (Tron Theatre); *The Tempest* and *What the Women Did* (Southwark Playhouse).
Dance designs include *Before the Tempest...After the Storm, Sophie/ Stateless* (Linbury, ROH); *Mixtures* (ENB / Westminster Abbey); *Non Exeunt* (Ballet Boyz/ Sadlers Wells).
Design for opera includes *The Queen of Spades* (Edinburgh Festival Theatre); *Cosi Fan Tutti* (British tour) and *King Arthur* (New Chamber Opera).
Forthcoming work includes *The Knot Garden* (Neue Oper Vienna); *Cymbeline* (Regent's Park); *In the Bag* (Traverse) and *Ghosts* (Linbury, ROH).

TIM MASCALL Lighting Designer

Recent lighting design credits include: *Vote Dizzy!* (Soho Theatre, London); *Why The Whales Came* (Comedy Theatre, London); *Off The Wall* (David Glass Ensemble UK Tour); *Filler Up!* (London, Washington DC, Montreal); *Passion* (Marie Forbes Dance Co, The Place Theatre, London); *Dazed* (Fracture Dance Theatre, Bloomsbury Theatre, London); *Testify* and *Cloudscape* (Middlesex University Dance Department); *The Sports Show 2004 / Main Arena* (Earl's Court, London); *When Harry Met Barry* (The Venue, London).
As an Associate Lighting Designer, Tim has worked with Chris Davey on *The Vagina Monologues* (UK tours and West End) and Matthew Eagland on *Little Women* (The Duchess Theatre, London).
Re-lights have included: *Home* (UK tour Oxford Stage Company); *My Boy Jack* (UK tour, Kenneth Wax Ltd / Hague Lang Productions); *The Lieutenant Of Inishmore* (UK tour); *Hay Fever* (UK tour, Oxford Stage Company); *Unheimlich Spine* (The David Glass Ensemble); *Plunge, To*

Time Taking Blush, *She is as He Eats*, *Inside Somewhere*, *Cranes*, *Playfall* and *Interlock* (all for Scottish Dance Theatre / Dundee Rep Theatre).
Other credits include sound designs for *After The Dance* (UK tour, Oxford Stage Company / Salisbury Playhouse), *The Cherry Orchard* (UK tour, Oxford Stage Company), *The Seagull*, *The Cherry Orchard*, and *The Futurists* (Drama Centre London).

ADRIENNE QUARTLY Sound Designer

Having studied music and become a Radio Producer for 5 years, Adrienne then gained a Master's Degree in Sound Design / Music for Performance at Central School of Speech and Drama in 2002. She now works as a freelance creative sound designer/composer in London. Productions include Quiconque's *Hideaway* (Complicité); *Lady Luck* (Lucy Porter at Assembly Rooms, Edinburgh 04); *Donkey Haughty* and *Attempts on Her Life* (BAC); *Jarman Garden* and *3 Women* (Riverside Studios); *Forgotten Voices* (Southwark Playhouse); *Habeas Corpus* and *Quartermaine's Terms* (Royal Theatre Northampton and Salisbury Playhouse); Circo Ridiculoso's *Inflated Ideas* (National Circus Bites Tour); *The Increased Difficulty of Concentration* and, most recently, *Woyzeck* and *Tejas Verdes* (Gate Theatre). Operating includes *Dumb Show* (Royal Court). As a cellist she is featured on Piano Magic's album *Artists Rifles*.

SALLYANN DICKSEE Costume Supervisor

Sallyann studied tailoring and pattern cutting at the London College of Fashion and took her first job at the Royal Opera House as a tailor and cutter. Following that she became a freelance wardrobe mistress and costume supervisor.
Theatre credits include *Mamma Mia* (London and Stuttgart); *His Dark Materials* (National Theatre); *Art* (David Pugh Ltd); *Life x 3* (David Pugh Ltd); *Up for Grabs* (Wyndhams Theatre) and *A Passionate Woman* (Comedy Theatre).
Music credits include *Bond*, *Geri Halliwell*.
Film & TV credits include *Clandestine Marriage*, *Harry Potter III*, *Stage Beauty*, *Pride and Prejudice*, *Vera Drake* and *Turn of the Screw* (BBC Wales).

ELEANOR GREEN Assistant Director

Eleanor is currently studying an MFA in Theatre Directing at Birkbeck, University of London. She has worked in London in theatre, film and TV production since graduating from UEA in 2000 with a BA in English and Drama. Directing credits include *The Zoo Story* by Edward Albee (Etcetera Theatre, Idiot Lamp Productions, 2004) and *Cigarettes and Chocolate* by Anthony Minghella, (assistant director, Sure Thing Productions, King's Head, 2004). Eleanor recently finished a 3-month placement at LAMDA.

ANNA JONES Assistant Designer

Anna trained on the Motley Theatre Design course. Since graduating last summer she has designed *The Biggleswades* at Southwark Playhouse, and assisted other designers including work on: *Tartuffe* (Arcola: designed by Jon Bausor); *Woyzeck* (Gate: designed by Neil Irish); and *A Night Just Before The Forest* (Arcola: designed by Patrick Burnier). Prior to Motley Anna studied drama at The University of Hull where she designed *The Hairy Ape, Weldon Rising* and *Puck.*

TOM ROGERS Assistant Designer

Following a Drama degree at Bristol University, Tom trained at Motley. Since graduating in July 2004, design work includes: Britten's *Let's Make An Opera / The Little Sweep* with director Will Kerley at the Benjamin Britten Festival, Aldeburgh; new opera *To the Edge* at the Steiner Theatre, Baker Street; *The Chimes* at Southwark Playhouse with artistic director Gareth Machin, and *Death and The Maiden* at the New Wolsey, Ipswich. He has assisted director David Edwards on Engelbert Humperdinck's *Hansel and Gretel* at the Proms 2004. Future projects include: Peter Brook's *The Man Who* at The Orange Tree, Richmond, and a touring production of Nick Darke's new play, *Laughing Gas.*

CHRIS UMNEY Production Manager

Since graduating from the Visual and Performing Arts (Theatre) BA course at Brighton University in 1995 Chris has been working as a composer, sound engineer, lighting designer and production manager for performance companies both in the UK and in Europe.

He has toured the UK with numerous companies including Sound & Fury, The People Show, Trio Con Brio, Voodoo Vaudeville, Quirk Productions, Bandbazi, Bright FX, Facepack Theatre, Intoto Theatre, Clout Dance Theatre, Barb Jungr and Brighton Theatre Events.

From 1994 to 1998 he was fortunate to work throughout Europe with the Brighton based Divas Dance Theatre Company and in 2001 Chris toured to 24 theatres in The Netherlands with Swamp Circus Theatre's production of *Moto.*

Most recently he worked as Production Manager on BAC's Christmas show *World Cup Final 1966* and designed the lighting for High Spin's touring performances of *Whodunnit?* and *Sleepwalker*, seen at the Hackney Empire in September 2004.

MARK ROSENBLATT Producer – Last Waltz Season

Mark is Artistic Director of Dumbfounded Theatre for whom he has directed CP Taylor's *Bread and Butter* at Southwark Playhouse, in a subsequent touring revival (co-produced with Oxford Stage Company) and at the Tricycle Theatre in 2004 (also with OSC).

Freelance work includes *The Taming of the Shrew* (Thelma Holt Ltd / Plymouth Theatre Royal and National tour); *The Tempest* (National

Theatre tour and Cottesloe); W Somerset Maugham's *The Circle* (for Oxford Stage Company and Salisbury Playhouse); two subsequent revivals of *The Circle*, one for Oxford Stage Company and one as a commercial tour starring Wendy Craig and Tony Britton (TEG / Yvonne Arnaud, Guildford); Kay Mellor's *A Passionate Woman* (Northampton Theatres); his own adaptation of S Anski's *The Dybbuk* (BAC) for which he received the James Menzies-Kitchin Young Director Award in 1999. Mark also directed BAFTA-nominated recordings of Shakespeare's *Romeo and Juliet, Hamlet, A Midsummer Night's Dream* and *Macbeth* for Kartouche Audio.

NEIL LAIDLAW Producer – Last Waltz Season

Neil is Producer for Dumbfounded Theatre and first worked with Mark Rosenblatt on the touring production of *Bread and Butter*. Originally from Scotland, he trained at the Royal Scottish Academy of Music and Drama. He has worked for many Scottish theatre companies, including Theatre by Design in their production of *Ghost Shirt* (Tron Theatre / Edinburgh Fringe) and Theatre Informer's Scottish tour of *Oleanna* by David Mamet. In 2002, he was awarded the prestigious Theatre Investment Fund / Society of London Theatre New Producers Bursary which allowed him to develop various projects over the year. Neil has most recently worked with Renard Company in a production at Glasgow's Tramway Theatre, and with early years theatre company Licketyspit. Neil is also producer for NML Productions, who recently co-produced *Sweet Phoebe* at the Byre Theatre, St Andrews.

Oxford Stage Company

'Oxford Stage Company has been one of the great success stories of recent years' The Daily Telegraph

Oxford Stage Company enjoys the freedom to produce work of great variety in a great variety of venues. From Stirling to the West End, we produce anything from drawing room classics to ambitious new plays. Our constant standard is to produce powerful and accomplished work that affects audiences anywhere, to return neglected classics to the popular repertoire and to present our work with wit and imagination and passion. We are also committed to giving opportunities to young artists and theatre workers, and to helping them increase their store of knowledge and experience. We are delighted by the opportunity to co-produce **The Last Waltz Season** at the Arcola. It fulfils all of our objectives. It also affords a wonderful insight into the hopes and the failings of Western Europe a hundred years ago.

Our goal is to develop a consistently exciting education and access programme to accompany our tours and to continue giving the best young directors, designers and actors an opportunity to work on a challenging larger scale.

Like most other arts organisations, we need to look for funding from every source to ensure that we thrive and grow. You can help us build on our vision to produce bold, timeless and relevant theatre by joining our Friends Scheme. Great theatre can only happen with Friends like you. With your support, we'll achieve even more.

If you would like to join our free mailing list or our friends scheme please contact us by phone on 020 7438 9946 or via email at info@oxfordstage.co.uk

For more information on future productions please go to our website www.oxfordstage.co.uk

Artistic Director	Dominic Dromgoole
Executive Producer	Henny Finch
Development Producer	Julia Hallawell
Associate Director	Sean Holmes
Finance and Administration Manager	Helen Hillman
Production and Tour Manager	Stephen Pamplin
Education Associate	Jacqui Somerville
Marketing and Administrative Assistant	Becky Pepper

OSC would like to thank all our Friends and especially our Favourites:
Muriel E B Quinn, John and Margaret Lynch and Uncle Honza.

Oxford Stage Company
Chertsey Chambers
12 Mercer Street
London WC2H 9QD

020 7438 9940
info@oxfordstage.co.uk

dumbfounded

Dumbfounded Theatre

Dumbfounded Theatre is a young company committed to the rediscovery of neglected work by outstanding European writers. Led by Mark Rosenblatt (Artistic Director) and Neil Laidlaw (Producer) it was formed in 2001 to stage a highly successful production of C P Taylor's *Bread and Butter* at Southwark Playhouse. *Bread and Butter* was subsequently revived in a touring co-production with Oxford Stage Company, and again at The Tricycle Theatre in 2004.

Future Projects: *Passages*

Samuel Adamson's newly commissioned play *Passages* (working title) intertwines three short stories by Nobel Prize-winning Yiddish novelist Isaac Bashevis Singer. *Passages* is being developed for production later this year.

Dumbfounded Theatre receives no core funding from Arts Council England or any other source. We raise funds on a project-to-project basis. We rely on the support of companies and individuals to allow us to develop our future plans. If you can help in any way please contact Neil Laidlaw on 020 8911 9276 or via email at info@dumbfounded.co.uk

Dumfounded Theatre Board:
Jennifer Cruickshank, Nia Janis, Rory Kinnear, Mark Rhodes and Emma Stenning.

Dumbfounded Theatre
60 Fellows Road
London NW3 3LJ
020 8911 9276 / 020 7483 2582
0870 460 1483 (f)
www.dumbfounded.co.uk

ROSE BERND

First published in this translation in 2005 by Oberon Books Ltd
521 Caledonian Road, London N7 9RH
Tel: 020 7607 3637 / Fax: 020 7607 3629
e-mail: oberon.books@btconnect.com
www.oberonbooks.com

A catalogue record for this book is available from the British
Library.

ISBN: 1 84002 551 4

Cover design: Pansy Aung and Winnie Wong

Characters

OLD BERND

ROSE BERND

MARTHEL

CHRISTOPH FLAMM

HENRIETTA FLAMM

ARTHUR STRECKMANN

AUGUST KEIL

FARM WORKERS:

HAHN

HEINZEL

GOLISCH

KLEINART

IN FLAMM'S SERVICE:

OLD MRS GOLISCH

HEAD MAIDSERVANT

A CONSTABLE

One

BERND's potato patch, by the cherry tree. A large crucifix at the side of the road. A May morning.

ROSE runs out of the bushes, flustered, excited. She sits. She notices one of her plaits has come undone. Reties it, quickly.

FLAMM comes out of the bushes.

Pause.

Sits, a considered distance from ROSE.

Pause.

They look at each other. Laugh.

Unable to contain himself, FLAMM stands up and sings wordlessly. She laughs more. He tries to get her to join in.

ROSE: Don't know the words, Mr Flamm.

FLAMM: Don't keep calling me Mr Flamm.

Sits back down with her.

ROSE: Congregation'll be out soon, Mr Flamm.

Beat.

FLAMM: Alright.

He stands and takes his gun out of a hollow in the tree.

Puts on gun, hat, takes out pipe.

Hat. Pipe.

Strikes a pose. She laughs.

Pause.

He notices cherries. Picks them. Offers some to ROSE.

Wild cherries, Rose.

She opens her mouth. He feeds her one.

I wish I was married to you, Rose.

Beat. She spits the stone onto the ground.

FLAMM: (*Going to touch her.*) Rosie –

ROSE: (*Pulling away.*) No.

Beat. She gives him her hand. He takes it.

FLAMM: Rose, I'm –

Beat.

Look, I'm the sort of –

Beat.

I…like my wife, I'm…

ROSE: Sink into the ground.

FLAMM: …very, very fond of her but…

This is different!

Beat. She giggles.

ROSE: Don't you go on, Mr Flamm.

FLAMM: Girl, you are a beautiful…maiden

She laughs.

…woman, alright, you are a beautiful…

Listen. It's strange this thing with me and my wife, it's complicated, it's…

Beat.

I mean Christ, what good is a cripple to me?

She pulls away. Beat.

ROSE: Congregation.

FLAMM: What do you keep going on about the congregation for?

ROSE: August's in church.

FLAMM: Creeps are always in church.

Look, I'm trying to tell you that you shouldn't worry too much about the wife.

ROSE: Can't look her in the eyes, sometimes, Christoph. Could just sink into the ground.

FLAMM: She's not stupid. See through brick walls that one.

Which is why if she ever found out about us…

Beat.

Well, it's not as if she'd tear our heads off.

No answer. She looks away.

Rose, what's so wrong with that?

Beat.

Rose? What's the matter?

ROSE: Been good to me, Christoph.

FLAMM: Good? I've been good to you?

I'm not fit for dog's meat.

Beat.

Look at me, Rose. I'm a mess.

Beat.

Could've been head forester to royalty by now. I'm not cut out for society. Even this is too civilised for me. Just want huts, guns, bear meat for dinner.

ROSE: Can't have what we want.

Beat.

Have to finish.

Pause.

FLAMM: Jesus Christ, won't there be enough left for that lovesick creep?

ROSE: Been waiting two years. Putting on the pressure now. Father wants it done.

Got to end.

FLAMM: You haven't even lived and now you want to strap yourself to that bookbinder? You've slaved away for your father, it's wrong working someone like a dog, it's…

Look, if that's all you want out of life, well there's time enough for that.

ROSE: Father's ill. Landlord's giving us notice, new tenant waiting to move in, the Father just wants things sorted before –

FLAMM: Then he should marry August Keil. If he's obsessed so with him.

Beat.

So the creep's saved a few shillings. That's no reason to go crawling into his paste-pot

ROSE: God don't want me hearing that. August's had problems. Illness, bad luck; hurt his soul.

FLAMM: 'Hurt his soul'? What does that mean? Go marry a convict if pity's a reason. Should stand up to the Father. So August grew up in an orphanage, but he's done alright. And if you don't take him they'll find him another. His brothers in the Lord are good at that sort of thing.

ROSE: No.

Not sorry for what's happened.

Can't go on.

FLAMM: What does that mean 'can't go on'?

ROSE: Things never change here. Not easy for me. Have pains in the chest sometimes…

Things have to change.

Beat.

FLAMM: Time I was getting back.

Gets up.

Can't do more now. Another time.

Bye, Rose.

She stares ahead.

What?

No other time?

Shakes her head.

Have I hurt you, Rose?

ROSE: So. Not like this, Mr Flamm. Not again.

Beat. He steps forward to touch her.

Someone's coming!

FLAMM looks.

Beat.

He grabs his stuff and leaves.

ROSE sorts herself out, picks up the hoe, begins on the potato patch.

STRECKMANN appears.

Pause.

He looks at her, then speaks as if he's only just noticed her.

STRECKMANN: ' Day, Rosie Bernd.

ROSE: ' Day, Streckmann.

Beat.

Where you come from? Church?

STRECKMANN: Left bit early.

ROSE: Really. Couldn't stand sermon, then?

STRECKMANN: Because it's so beautiful out here. Left the wife inside. Have to have moments to yourself once in a while, Rose Bernd.

ROSE: Rather be in church.

STRECKMANN: Well. 'S'where women belong.

ROSE: Probably got sins enough clinging to your soul. Do well to pray.

STRECKMANN: On good terms with the Lord our God. Don't take such close interest in my sins.

ROSE: Really.

STRECKMANN: Don't bother himself much gazing at me.

ROSE: Conceited.

STRECKMANN laughs.

Real man don't beat his wife.

STRECKMANN: Really? But that's right. That's proper, that is. Have to be shown who's boss.

ROSE: Don't imagine any such stupidity.

STRECKMANN: This is how it is; what's right remains right. And I like to get what I want.

Pause.

They say you want to leave Flamm's service.

Beat.

ROSE: No longer in Flamm's service, can't your eyes see me doing other things?

STRECKMANN: Helping at Flamm's yesterday.

ROSE: Help or don't help, why do you care?

STRECKMANN: True that your father's moved?

ROSE: Where then?

STRECKMANN: In with August at the Lachmann's house.

ROSE: August hasn't even bought the house yet, know more than I do.

STRECKMANN: Heard you're getting married soon.

ROSE: Let them keep talking.

Pause. STRECKMANN comes close.

STRECKMANN: 'S'right. Can marry whenever, fine girl like you can enjoy herself a little first.

He watches her.

Nobody believes him.

I laughed in his face.

ROSE: Who?

STRECKMANN: August Keil.

Beat. She carries on working.

Bit touchy, is August.

ROSE: Not interested in your quarrels, one of you's no better than the other.

STRECKMANN: Really? What about as far as boldness goes?

ROSE: Already know about your boldness. Just need to listen to women.

STRECKMANN: (*Laughing.*) Am I denying it?

ROSE: Couldn't.

STRECKMANN: 'S'not good to eat cherries with me, girl. What I want from a woman, I get.

ROSE: Really?

STRECKMANN: Really. How much would you bet on it, Rosie? Seen you looking.

ROSE: Don't go imagining such –

He reaches out to touch her hair.

(*Pulling away.*) Streckmann! Told you, keep your hands back.

Beat.

STRECKMANN: What am I doing to you then?

Pause. He watches her.

You'll come running one of these days. Can play the innocent all you like: see that cross? Done stuff in my time, but under a cross? Be ashamed. What would your father say? What would August say? Now, I could've swore there was a gun in the hollow of this tree…

ROSE: What?

STRECKMANN: Nothing.

I'm saying nothing. But when someone's not doing nothing, not thinking nothing and then someone like you starts accusing –

ROSE: What's that mean; someone like me?

STRECKMANN: Got no special meaning.

ROSE is furious but can say nothing. STRECKMANN laughs.

Look, don't make a meal out of it, just how things are. Now, what d'you think I am, Rosie Bernd? What's it matter to me? The best women are the ones who get away with it. Man like me knows. Always known about you, Rosie Bernd.

ROSE: Get away from this patch! I'm… There'll be an accident! I'll…

STRECKMANN sits down.

STRECKMANN: Weeping and wailing? (*Imitating.*) Christ's spit, no, no!

Think I'll go running off telling on you? Gossiping on you? How's it hurt me, what you get up to?

ROSE: I'll hang myself from a beam! Marielle Schubert did.

STRECKMANN: Things were different there, she'd broken different commandments. And I had nothing to do with that. Anyway, not something to go hanging yourself for or there'd be no women left, just how it is. How it is everywhere. We sit where we sit.

Beat.

I had to laugh, though…Your father carrying himself so high in the air. Stares right through you, like you should beg death, because perhaps you've gone a little astray. Well: should keep better eye on his own livestock…

She starts saying the Lord's Prayer.

Is that not right? Swallowed piety by the spoon load, August Keil, the Father, and you. I cannot stand piety.

ROSE: Liar. You didn't see –

STRECKMANN: What? What didn't I see? Hold on a minute: I must've been dreaming. That's what it must've been. Wasn't that the Magistrate Flamm – and I haven't touched a drop today, Rosie – and wasn't he riding you by your plaits? Throw you down in the grass? Good grip he had on you, alright.

ROSE: I'll crack your head with this!

STRECKMANN: (*Laughing.*) No need to get all rough, girl. Why shouldn't you do it? Don't blame you, first come, first served, it's the same here.

ROSE: Someone like you –

STRECKMANN: But where Flamm fits, so do I.

She stares at him, shocked.

ROSE: Been decent all this life! Cared for three small brothers and sisters, out at three in the morning without a drop of milk! People know this! Every child knows this!

STRECKMANN: Then you don't need to make such a song and dance about it – congregation's coming from the church. Just be a bit friendly, is all. You people and your pride: you could burst with it.

But you're no better than anyone else.

ROSE: August?

STRECKMANN: Where? That's nice, the two of them walking by the parson's garden…

Well? What then? You think I should go? Not afraid of praying donkeys.

ROSE: Streckmann, I've saved up twelve –

STRECKMANN: Rosalina, you'll've saved a bit more than that.

ROSE: Alright. Give you what I have, throw it all in, Streckmann, but please –

STRECKMANN: I don't want your money!

ROSE: Streckmann, please –

STRECKMANN: Just wanna see you come to your senses.

Beat.

ROSE: If the village hears –

STRECKMANN: Up to you. Nobody needs to know. You don't speak no-one'll know.

Well?

You been in my mind, girl –

ROSE: Which woman isn't in your mind?

STRECKMANN: That's fair enough. Someone like me, going round with that threshing machine, all estates round the country doesn't get scared of being gossiped at. But I know how I feel, Rose. Before Flamm showed up – not mentioning August – I'd noticed you. What I felt…

But if the devil's going to take me it'll be arse first! What comes, comes, Rosie! No more messing: I saw something today.

ROSE: What was it then?

STRECKMANN: You know.

MARTHEL enters, Sunday best.

MARTHEL: Rose, that you? What you doing?

Beat.

ROSE: I'm –

I'm finishing this patch? Why d'you leave it like this?

MARTHEL: Rose, it's Sunday, if Father sees you –

STRECKMANN: If there's profit in it, he won't bite your head off, one thing we know of Old Bernd.

MARTHEL: Who's that, Rosla?

ROSE: Don't question.

OLD BERND and AUGUST enter, Sunday best, prayer books.

BERND: That Rosla?

AUGUST: Yes, Father Bernd.

BERND: Can't stop her, August. Mood takes her, she has to go slaving away, weekday, holy-day…

Not enough time in the week for you, girl?

AUGUST: You are working too much, Rose. That's not necessary.

BERND: Pastor saw you it'd hurt his soul, think his eyes liars.

AUGUST: Asked after you again, Rose.

STRECKMANN: Maybe he wants to take her in his service.

BERND: Streckmann?

STRECKMANN: (*Coming forward.*) Every inch of me. Hardworking girl; goes at it like a…ant. Even if the weight of it cracks her ribs. She's no time for sleeping in your church.

BERND: We two hardly slept there. Think it's those out here who sleep and don't want to be woken. The bridegroom is near at hand…

STRECKMANN: That is true as it's written. The bride, however, appears to be missing.

AUGUST: You're in a very droll mood.

STRECKMANN: 'S'right. I could kiss a curb-stone, August, or perhaps the handle of your collection bag. I feel most unusually cheerful. I could puke with laughter.

BERND: Get your things, we're going home – but not like that! Hide that hoe in the cherry tree. Walking with you holding that leave us shamed.

AUGUST: There are those that carry guns on Sundays.

STRECKMANN: Some little imps can even be seen carrying bottles of schnapps.

Takes out bottle of schnapps.

AUGUST: Every man must accounts for his own actions.

STRECKMANN: 'S'right. And for the expense too. Come on, be brave and have a drink.

Offers the bottle. AUGUST is still. Pause.

BERND: You know August doesn't drink Schnapps.

Where's your threshing machine?

STRECKMANN: Machine's on the estate. You'll have a drop, Father Bernd? You were a distiller yourself once.

BERND: (*Taking bottle.*) As it's you, Streckmann, rather not, though. Was manager on the estate had to do it all, but I'd've preferred not to have made schnapps, and I never drank it. In those days.

STRECKMANN: (*To AUGUST who is putting the hoe in the cherry tree.*) Look at that cherry tree. BANG! Could just take aim and let fly.

BERND: There's people hunt on Sundays.

STRECKMANN: Magistrate Flamm.

BERND: Just met him. 'S'bad. Feel sorry for people like that.

STRECKMANN is throwing cockchafers at ROSE.

ROSE: Streckmann!

AUGUST: What are you doing?

STRECKMANN: Nothing.

We have a private quarrel..

AUGUST: Pick your quarrels where you like, but I'd rather you left this one alone.

STRECKMANN: Take care, August. Watch yourself.

BERND: Peace! Be friendly, in the name of Our Saviour.

STRECKMANN: That corpse is always at me.

AUGUST: A corpse is something that's in a grave.

Beat.

STRECKMANN: August, let's be nice. The Father's right, be friendly to each other. Not Christian the way you're behaving: have a drink. You may not be pretty but you know your way around reading and writing and you've brought your lambs in out of the rain. Be getting yourself happily married, soon. Come on, drink.

STRECKMANN holds out the bottle. AUGUST makes no move, so Father BERND takes it and drinks.

I appreciate that, Father Bernd.

BERND: To a happy marriage!

STRECKMANN: Exactly. That's civil, Father. That's right thing to do. Not like when I was groom on the big estate anymore is it, when you had me under the whip. I'm reputable now. Man with a head can make his way.

BERND: If the Lord extends his grace to him, yes. (*To AUGUST.*) Drink with us to the happy wedding.

AUGUST: (*Taking the bottle.*) God's to give, we don't have to drink to it.

STRECKMANN: (*Laughing.*) And may he give you lots of little Augusts, so grandfather'll be happy! (*AUGUST drinks.*) And maybe the first one out'll be a magistrate. Let Rosla drink to that.

BERND: What's matter Rosla, crying?

MARTHEL: Tears always falling out of her eyes.

AUGUST: (*To ROSE.*) Let him have his way; drink.

Reluctantly she takes she bottle. Drinks. Disgusted.

STRECKMANN: Chop, chop, get it inside you, girl.

She hands the bottle back to AUGUST.

BERND: (*Joking to STRECKMANN, but with pride.*) There's a girl, eh! Better keep a good grip on her when they're wed!

Two

FLAMM's House. MRS FLAMM in her wheelchair, reading. Looks out the window. Nothing. Goes back to her book. Reads.

Pause. She listens. Closes her book.

MRS FLAMM: (*Calling out.*) Just come in!

Pause.

Timid Knock.

Well?

OLD BERND's head appears.

Is this our Parish Councillor and Trustee of the orphanage? Come in, Father Bernd, and I'll try not to bite you.

BERND: We would have a conversation with the Lieutenant.

He enters, followed by AUGUST. Both are wearing their best clothes. She takes this in.

MRS FLAMM: Well. This looks very serious.

BERND: Good morning to you, Mrs Flamm.

MRS FLAMM: My husband was in the hunting room. Is this your son-in-law?

BERND: Lord allows.

MRS FLAMM: So you're here to make the arrangements? At last.

Beat.

BERND: Yes. Thanks to God, we're ready now.

MRS FLAMM: Her mind is made up?

BERND: And a rock has been taken out of my soul. Took her time, but now she can't wait, would rather wedding were today than tomorrow.

MRS FLAMM: Congratulations, Keil. I'm pleased for you Father Bernd.

(*Calling.*) Christel?

No answer.

My husband will be here soon.

They wait. Awkward.

So. You must be very pleased with yourself, Father Bernd.

Beat.

BERND: Exactly how it is, Mrs Flamm. Had a good talk the day before yesterday, decided it all. And now God hands us even more plenty; August went to see Lady Gnadau and she's lent him three thousand so that he can buy the Lachmann's place.

MRS FLAMM: Really?

Well. That's…

Well, there you are, Father Bernd. You despaired when your master let you go without a pension, but now it appears that God is taking care of you after all.

BERND: Men never have enough faith.

MRS FLAMM: Nicely set up now; house opposite the church, good piece of land with it. You can be really satisfied.

Beat.

BERND: The happiness a lady like that can bestow, next to our saviour it's her we have to thank the most. Only I'd been in Lady Gnadau's service, eaten away at the health for her as I did for my master, I'd have no cause for complaint.

MRS FLAMM: You have no cause for complaint now, Bernd.

BERND: No, no, definitely not. Certainly not. In one way, no.

MRS FLAMM: There's no gratitude in this world. My father was head forester for forty years, but when he died we still lived in want.

You have an excellent son-in-law, nice house, land to work on, can let your children look after you now, see to it that you prosper.

BERND: What I hope for. Have no doubts. Man who's made his way by handling documents...

MRS FLAMM: Didn't you want to be a missionary, Keil?

AUGUST: Body was too weak.

BERND: ...by writing, reading, well as by his trade, God-fearing, Christian, upright man –

MRS FLAMM: But my husband is giving up his duties here, I don't think he'll be able to certify the marriage.

BERND: But they're in a hurry –

MRS FLAMM: I know, I know that, Bernd. I've already had Rose here this morning.

(*Calling.*) Christel!

FLAMM: (*Off.*) Present and correct!

MRS FLAMM: (*Calling.*) Registry business.

FLAMM enters, cleaning a shotgun, no jacket or waistcoat, shirt open.

FLAMM: Alright, alright. Been with Streckmann trying to sort out the threshing, but he says the machine's up on the estate –

Christ. Father Bernd.

BERND: Yes, Mr Flamm. We have come because we were wanting –

FLAMM: Patience! One thing after another.

Examining the barrels of the gun.

Look, Father Bernd, if you have registry business you'd do better to wait. Steckle is to be my successor and he's bound to be better at all this than me.

MRS FLAMM: Christel, what are you talking about?

AUGUST: (*Coming forward, agitated.*) Your honour, we wish to make announcement of a marriage.

Beat.

With God's help I have become ready to enter into a state of holy matrimony.

FLAMM: Then what's the hurry?

MRS FLAMM: What concern is it of yours, Christel? Stop preaching and let them marry in peace. If he had his way, Father Bernd, the entire village would be single.

FLAMM: Marriage is for the stupid.

Beat.

You the bookbinder? August Keil?

AUGUST: I am.

FLAMM: Just bought the Lachmann house?

AUGUST: I…have.

FLAMM: Starting a bookshop?

AUGUST: A book and stationary shop, yes. Probably.

BERND: He's thinking principally of devotional publications.

FLAMM: There's land with the Lachmann House, isn't there? By the pear tree.

BERND & AUGUST: Yes.

Beat.

FLAMM: Then we're neighbours.

Puts down his gun, starts searching for his keys.

(*Calling.*) Minna!

MAID enters.

Wheel your mistress out.

He sits at the table.

MRS FLAMM: Such chivalry.

You're right, I am in the way. Girl, take me into the hunting room.

(*To the MAID as they go.*) Sort your hair out.

Beat.

FLAMM: Feel sorry for the Lachmanns. Got it at a knock-down price, did you?

AUGUST coughs, embarrassed.

What's the difference. Should congratulate yourselves.

So. You want to –

Where's the bride.

Beat.

Is she reluctant?

AUGUST: We are in absolute agreement, I think.

BERND: 'll go fetch her, Sir.

BERND exits. FLAMM opens his desk, roots around.

FLAMM: (*Muttering.*) Stupid. What's the hurry?

Pause.

Well, do what you want. I'm gonna smoke.

Fills pipe. Lights it. Smokes.

D'you smoke, Keil?

AUGUST: No.

FLAMM: Take snuff?

AUGUST: No.

FLAMM: Don't drink beer, schnapps, wine?

AUGUST: Communion wine.

FLAMM: Iron principles. Fantastic.

Come in!

Beat.

Did someone knock?

No answer.

No?

Must've been…

Pause. FLAMM smokes.

Heard you do quack doctoring?

AUGUST shakes his head, shocked.

Thought I heard you healed with prayer?

AUGUST: That would be something quite different from quack doctoring.

FLAMM: Really?

AUGUST: Faith can move mountains. And what we ask for of the Lord in a spirit that is pure…

Our Father is almighty still and with us today even as –

FLAMM: Come in!

Beat.

Did someone just knock?

Come in! Come in, for Christ's sake!

OLD BERND brings in a reluctant ROSE. Pause.

Good.

Long pause.

Wait here.

He goes into the hunting room. They speak in whispers.

BERND: What was Streckmann saying?

ROSE: Who?

BERND: Streckmann was outside, talking to her.

ROSE: What's he s'posed to have said, then?

BERND: 'S'what I'm asking!

ROSE: Don't know!

AUGUST: Should have nothing to do with someone like that.

ROSE: Can I do if someone speaks to me?

BERND: So he did speak to you!

ROSE: If he did, didn't listen.

BERND: Should report that Streckmann, make complaint against him. Going past his threshing machine, he called something out after us. Couldn't hear the words…

AUGUST: If a woman speaks two words to him then her good name is blackened.

ROSE: Oh…go find a better girl, then.

FLAMM re-enters, properly dressed.

FLAMM: Well.

When d'you want this wedding?

No answer.

What's the matter?

No answer.

Are you not in agreement?

Look, why don't you go home and sleep on it. When you decide you can come back –

AUGUST: The matter must be seen to now!

FLAMM: Alright, Keil, I'm not saying otherwise!

FLAMM starts taking notes.

Well?

BERND: Soon as is possible, is what we thought.

AUGUST: Four, five weeks.

FLAMM: So Soon?

AUGUST: Yes, Mr Flamm.

FLAMM: Well, can I have a date? I mean, these things take time, it's –

ROSE: Maybe it could do with more time.

Beat. They stare at her.

FLAMM: Rosie, what do you mean?

Rose, I mean…Rose. Known each other since so long, it's…

Well.

It seems she's not in agreement.

Beat.

AUGUST: Goodbye and good health, Father Bernd.

BERND: Stay where you are, August!

(*To ROSE.*) You make a choice now! D'you understand?

Three days ago you gave me the sacred promise to wed this man, couldn't wait for the day, and now you don't want to know? Who do you think you are? Think yourself special because you're decent, hardworking, no-one to say evil to you? There's other girls don't go to dances, they're not all sluts and whores because you're pious! Any different you'd've been on the street, girl, no daughter of mine! This man here don't need you, this man, man like this need only reach out the little finger to have a pile of women, finest blood. Patience is snapped! Arrogance! Pride, vanity! If you don't fulfil your promise now –

FLAMM: Steady, Father Bernd…

BERND: You don't know, your honour! Girl wants to play with this kind of man, no daughter of mine!

AUGUST: Why do you hate me? What have I done to you? I knew this couldn't work, I'm marked for misfortune, how many times have I said that to you, Father Bernd, that I'm marked for misfortune.

Nevertheless. Been honest, worked hard and God has been kind insomuch as he hasn't made things any worse. No family in that orphanage, no brothers or sisters, only our saviour to cling to, but this thing isn't meant for me, oh no, because that would be too much like something good in my life. I know I'm not the most handsome man but I asked and you said yes! God sees into your heart!

Tries to go but BERND stops him.

BERND: Wait, please!

(*To ROSE.*) This man was my support long before he asked to wed you. Ill, earning nothing, nobody cared but he came and broke his bread with us

AUGUST storms out.

like an angel of the Lord, he –

August?

ROSE: I'm willing, just want...time.

BERND: Three years! Three years, girl!

Well, you can fend for yourself, now.

He leaves.

FLAMM: Well, well.

He closes the register, looks at ROSE.

Rose?

No answer.

Look, you don't want to take all that fire and brimstone seriously, it's –

ROSE is shivering.

Rose, come on.

Pause.

Alright, then.

Does little things, distracted.

Rose?

(*Whispers.*) Meet me behind the outbuildings. Rose? I have to talk to you about all this. She's in the hunting room, can't do it here.

ROSE: Never again, Mr Flamm.

Beat.

FLAMM: Are you possessed or something? Been running round for four weeks trying to speak to you, behave like I'm a leper. And what happens? This happens.

ROSE: Deserve no better, keep wiping your boots on me, but –

FLAMM: (*Striking the table.*) Jesus Christ!

ROSE steps back, shocked. They stare at each other.

MRS FLAMM in her wheelchair, pushed in by the MAID.

MRS FLAMM: Flamm?

Beat. FLAMM storms out. MRS FLAMM turns to ROSE.

What's wrong with him?

ROSE is trying not to cry, but fails.

MRS FLAMM: What…

Girl, what's the matter?

I don't understand, you're like a different person, what's
–

(*To the maid.*) Tidy the kitchen.

MAID exits.

Well? Are you in trouble or…

What are you saying?

No answer.

Look, tell me and you'll feel better.

Don't you want to marry this pasty August? Rose? Is
there someone else, girl? Well listen to me; each man is
worth as much as the next and none of them are worth
that much.

ROSE controls herself.

ROSE: Know what I should do.

Definitely.

Beat.

MRS FLAMM: Oh? Well, you're alright then. It's just that I
got the impression that you didn't.

ROSE is no longer crying. MRS FLAMM looks at her.

Rosie…

Are you perhaps unwell?

ROSE: Unwell? How d'you mean?

MRS FLAMM: Just unwell.

ROSE: Not unwell.

MRS FLAMM: I'm not saying you are. Just asking.

Beat.

No games, Rose, I don't want to play hide and seek.

D'you think I want to hurt you?

ROSE shakes her head.

MRS FLAMM: Good.

You used to play with my Kurt, grew up side by side. Until God took him from me.

Then you lost your mother. She asked me to look after you.

ROSE: Should throw myself into the lake. That happens, Jesus Lord, forgive the sin.

MRS FLAMM: If that happens – ?

Beat. MRS FLAMM looks at her.

Does anyone know?

No answer.

Take me to that chest of drawers.

ROSE does so.

Your mother once said to me, 'My Rose was born to be the mother of children, but her blood…it's too hot.' I don't know.

MRS FLAMM takes a doll from the drawer.

But being a mother is not to be despised. You and Kurtel used to play with this doll, but it was you that did the looking after. Washed her, fed her, changed her, Flamm said he once saw you with the doll to your breast.

You put flowers on Kurt's grave on Sunday, didn't you?
Again. Children and graves are women's matters.

Has taken out a child's linen shift.

Your father has his missions and bible lessons and such
things, says everyone's a sinner, wants to turn them into
angels. Could be right, don't know. But I do know one
thing; what a mother is here on this earth, and how she is
blessed with agony.

Lays dress in ROSE's lap.

Go home and be happy. I won't ask you anymore, we
must be extra careful, that's all. I don't need to know
anything, believe me, I don't care who the father is,
whether he's a viscount or a vagrant. It's the women who
bring children into this world, and no-one helps us with
that.

I'll think it all through properly.

At least I'm good for something.

ROSE: No. Can't take help.

Don't deserve it.

See it through on my own.

You're like an angel, God in his eternity, you are too
good...but I can't accept.

Gives dress back and goes to leave.

MRS FLAMM: I can't let you go like this, Rose, I don't
know what you might do.

ROSE: Don't worry. Long way from the end now, Mrs
Flamm. Needs be, can work for the child. Big world. Was
just me, wasn't for the father and didn't feel so much pity
for August...

But then a child should have a father.

MRS FLAMM: Then why are you fighting this wedding?

ROSE: What to say? Don't know. Don't want to fight,
except…Streckmann…

Pause.

MRS FLAMM: Be open with me, understand?

Well, you can go home now, if you like. Come back
tomorrow. And listen to me; be happy! A woman should
be happy of a child.

ROSE: God knows I am. I'll see it through, but…can't have
no-one help me with it.

She leaves. MRS FLAMM picks up the dress.

MRS FLAMM: Well, girl, it's a piece of good fortune you
have, for a woman. Cherish it.

Three

By the pear tree, early August. A spring flows into a stone basin. Distant hum of the threshing machine.

Enter BERND and AUGUST, hot and tired.

BERND: Hot and more today! Need rest, but it's the pleasure, working your own land.

AUGUST: I'm not used to this mowing.

BERND: Handled yourself well.

AUGUST: My limbs are twitching and cramping.

BERND: Done well. Men get used to this kind of work, and for you it'll be the exception. You could easily be a gardener.

AUGUST: For a day, then I'd collapse. It's my condition. Went to the doctor again; same as always, he just shrugs his shoulders.

BERND: Better off in the hands of the Almighty. Couple of rusty nails in a cup of water, two or three weeks, then drink the solution, that's the most you should do.

Silence.

Hope this weather holds.

AUGUST: Heat's killing me. Thought I heard thunder.

BERND lays down and drinks

BERND: Water is the best drink.

AUGUST: What's the time?

BERND: Must be four. Where's Rose with our meal?

BERND inspects the blade of his scythe. AUGUST copies.

Have to hone? Mine'll last.

AUGUST: I...can try like this for a bit more.

BERND: (*Sitting.*) Sit by me here, and if you have testament with you, perhaps you could edify us with a little.

AUGUST: (*Sitting, exhausted.*) I'll just say God be praised and thanked and leave it at that.

Pause.

BERND: 'Let her be,' I said. 'Girl'll find her way.' You see, August? Come to the senses now. As God breathes, though, like she was running up against an invisible wall. Just had to find her way around.

AUGUST: Don't know what got into her that day. I mean, what was it all about? Still can't work it out.

BERND: Not like that this time, though...

AUGUST: Glad 's'no longer Magistrate Flamm.

BERND: ...didn't bat an eyelid this time, four, five minutes, all sorted, arrangements, paperwork, everything. How she is sometimes, just how the women are.

Beat.

AUGUST: Think it had something to do with Streckmann? Was talking to her that time. And he called something after you as well.

BERND: Maybe, maybe not, can't get nothing out of her. Pleased she's getting a husband who'll influence her against sullenness.

AUGUST: When I see engineer Streckmann, it's like I'm looking at the Evil One.

BERND: Maybe she thought he was up to something. Been capable of mischief since he was a child.

AUGUST: When I see that man, I don't know myself anymore. I get hot and cold flushes and I want to complain against our Heavenly Father, because he didn't make me a Sampson. Then – God forgive me – I have bad thoughts.

Beat. Whistle of the thresher.

That'll be him.

BERND: Don't take the notice of him.

AUGUST: No. When it's over, I'll close myself up in four walls and then we'll have the quiet life.

BERND: The beautiful quiet life, God grant.

AUGUST: And I won't want anything more of this world. Detest the whole thing! Have such a loathing of the world and humanity, Father…it rises like bile into my throat. Then I laugh. I think of the peace of dying and I laugh like a child.

Beat.

Farm workers enter from FLAMM's; HAHN, HEINZEL, GOLISCH, his wife OLD MRS GOLISCH, KLEINART and the HEAD MAID.

HAHN: (*Running.*) Always first to the spring!

He kneels at the spring.

Like to jump straight in –

HEAD MAID: You dare! I'm thirsty. Hang on, Head Maid comes first.

HEINZEL: (*Pushing between them.*) Men come first, then shes.

KLEINART: Room there for all – that right, Father Bernd?

T'your meal.

BERND: Only there is no meal. Waiting here in vain.

GOLISCH: Sweating enough to be wrung out. The tongue's like a chunk of charred wood in the mouth.

MRS GOLISCH: Water!

KLEINART: Enough for everyone.

They drink, some from cups, some from hats, some directly from the surface.

HEINZEL: Water's good, but beer'd be better.

HAHN: Or a little brandy.

GOLISCH: August'll stand us a quart.

MRS GOLISCH: Better invite us to the wedding.

GOLISCH: We'll all be going. Meant to be soon.

HEINZEL: I'm not going.

What for? Drink cold water? Can do that here.

HAHN: Praying and singing for pudding. Who knows, maybe we'll be treated to the pastor from Jenkau asking us if we know the ten commandments.

HEINZEL: Or even the seven beatitudes. Wouldn't be good; forgotten it all.

Laughter.

KLEINART: Leave August alone. Tell you, I had such a girl, couldn't wish for a better son-in-law. Knows what he's doing, the eyes are open and you always know where he is.

They eat, chunks of bread and coffee from tin pots.

MRS GOLISCH: There's Rosie, from round that barn.

GOLISCH: Look at that girl gallop.

KLEINART: Carry a sack of wheat upstairs on her own, that girl. Saw her taking a wardrobe on a barrow to the new home this morning. Girls got meat and bone. She'll manage that house.

HAHN: If I could do like August, swear my soul, people, I wouldn't mind; I'd give piety a go.

GOLISCH: Have to learn to chase success before you can catch it.

HAHN: Remember him tramping round villages selling tracts from his bag, writing letters for people? Now he's got the tastiest property in the district and can wed the tastiest girl.

Enter ROSE with the evening meal.

ROSE: T'your meal!

OTHERS: T'your meal, t'your meal. Thank you.

GOLISCH: Letting the sweetheart starve, Rosie?

ROSE: Don't think he starves that easy.

HEINZEL: Feed him up, Rosie, or you won't get any meat on him.

GOLISCH: Won't be enough of him to get a grip on

BERND: Where've you been? Been waiting half the hour.

AUGUST: (*Quiet but annoyed.*) Now they're all here! Could've been finished and gone long ago.

MRS GOLISCH: Let him groan, girl, don't mind it.

ROSE: Who's groaning, Mrs Golisch? Nothing to groan about, August wouldn't dream of groaning.

MRS GOLISCH: Even so. Just saying you shouldn't take it seriously.

HEINZEL: Don't groan now, it'll come later.

ROSE: Not afraid it'll ever come.

GOLISCH: You're very understanding together all of a sudden.

ROSE: Me and August always understood each other.

She kisses him. The others laugh.

What's funny. Always like this.

GOLISCH: Really? It's just I was imagining I might be climbing in through her window one day…

KLEINART: Be carrying your bones home in a handkerchief!

HEAD MAID: Oh dear, dear me! I'd try give her a go, though; never know…

BERND: (*Serious calm.*) Take care, Head Maid.

KLEINART: Listen to this; take care! Old Bernd can't take a joke!

ROSE: Don't mean nothing, let her be.

KLEINART: Looks as mild as the lamb now, but when he lets fly, you wouldn't believe it. I remember when he was manager of the estate; women didn't laugh then. Sort out ten of you and no time for messing with the boys then.

HEAD MAID: Who's messing with boys?

KLEINART: Better ask engineer Streckmann.

HEAD MAID: (*Crimson.*) You can ask Jesus Christ himself, for all I care!

STRECKMANN appears, dusty, drunk.

STRECKMANN: Who wants engineer Streckmann? Here he is, standing in front of you.

Beat.

Good afternoon people. T'your meal.

MRS GOLISCH: Talk of the devil and he shall appear…

STRECKMANN: And you're the devil's grandmother.

He takes off his cap, wipes his brow.

Not working here again; this slavery strips your skin and bones. 'Day August, 'day Rosie, 'day Father Bernd.

Beat.

Jesus Christ, can't you speak?

HEINZEL: Some people're too well off.

STRECKMANN: God hands it to his own when they're sleeping. Men like me slave and still get nowhere.

He squeezes himself between HEINZEL and KLEINART, produces a schnapps bottle, hands it to HEINZEL

Pass it round.

MRS GOLISCH: Got it best, Streckmann, what you got to moan about? God's sake, you earn two or three times our money for standing next to a machine.

STRECKMANN: Got a mind, I want brain work! You straw-heads don't understand, what do old women know? I got troubles.

GOLISCH: Streckmann's got troubles, Lord!

STRECKMANN: More than enough! Needle sticking in my belly, into the soul…makes me feel so shitty-arsed I might do something bad.

Want me to come lie over there, Head Maid?

HEAD MAID: If you want your head hit with a whetstone.

GOLISCH: That's what his trouble is; everything goes dark, can't see, suddenly he's in bed with a girl.

They laugh.

STRECKMANN: Laugh, cripples. Puke yourself laughing. I got nothing to laugh at. I feel like sticking my arm in that machine, let the piston rip right through me.

HAHN: Maybe you should set the barn alight.

STRECKMANN: There's fire enough in here! Now, August…there's a happy man.

AUGUST: Happy, not happy, that's nothing to no-one.

STRECKMANN: What am I doing to you? Could be sociable.

AUGUST: I seek my society elsewhere.

Beat. STRECKMANN grabs the Schnapps.

STRECKMANN: Give! Troubles should be drowned. (*To ROSE.*) Don't watch me. Deal's a deal.

He gets up.

Off. Don't want to come between.

ROSE: Go or stay, I don't care.

MRS GOLISCH: (*Innocently.*) What was that you said then, Streckmann? Three weeks ago, by the threshing machine?

Beat. Suddenly the workers bust out laughing.

STRECKMANN: Nothing. Don't know what you're on about.

MRS GOLISCH: Knew enough then.

KLEINART: You lot, stop your gossiping.

MRS GOLISCH: Shouldn't be talking so big all the time, then.

STRECKMANN: (*Coming back.*) What I say I'll do, I'll do, shit if I don't! Enough; not saying more.

MRS GOLISCH: Just as easy to do that with your mouth closed.

Coming back again, restraining himself.

STRECKMANN: Never mind! Not jumping into your trap. You want to know more, ask August, or Father Bernd there.

BERND: What? What are we supposed to know?

MRS GOLISCH: That time you went to Flamm's…You passed Streckmann and he called something out after you.

KLEINART: Quiet, now!

MRS GOLISCH: Why? He was just joking…whether you were all agreed or whether Rosie needed persuading.

BERND: God, forgive them their sin! Why can't you leave us in peace? What have we done to you?

MRS GOLISCH: Not doing nothing.

ROSE: Don't worry yourselves about what I wanted or didn't, today I want and that's all.

KLEINART: Good for you, Rosie.

AUGUST: (*Has had his head in his bible the whole time, now closing it.*) Come on, Father. To work.

HAHN: Bit more sweat than sticking together prayer books or stirring your paste-pot, eh August?

HEINZEL: 'S'after the wedding, that's when he'll sweat. Girl like Rosie has demands.

Laughter. Joining in, STRECKMANN goes to say something, but seeing ROSE, stops himself.

STRECKMANN: Jesus! Nearly said something I shouldn't, then.

(*Coming back.*) Leave you a riddle, shall I? Still waters run deep; you should never taste blood, because it just gets worse and worse – the thirst for it.

MRS GOLISCH: What? When did you taste blood?

BERND: That probably means brandy.

STRECKMANN: On my way. Don't worry, I'll be good. Bye Father Bernd. Bye August. Bye Rosie…

Beat.

What's matter? Don't you get above yourself, August. It's alright, don't worry, you won't see much more of me. But you've got grounds for thanking me. You've always been full of spite, but I've made an agreement, I have given my consent and everything'll run smooth.

He leaves.

ROSE: Let him talk, August.

KLEINART: Flamm's here.

Looks at his watch.

Been over the half hour.

The whistle of the machine is heard.

HAHN: Forward, Prussians! Misery calls.

They leave except for AUGUST, BERND and ROSE.

BERND: Sodom and Gomorrah was here! Spew from Streckmann!

Beat.

D'you understand it Rose?

ROSE: Got better things to think on.

Taps AUGUST on the head.

That right, August? No time for stupidity, have work to do over these next six weeks.

She begins to clear the stuff away.

AUGUST: Come over later.

ROSE: Have to wash, iron, sew buttonholes. Getting close now.

BERND: 'll be back for supper after seven.

BERND goes. AUGUST watches ROSE.

AUGUST: D'you love me, Rosie?

ROSE: (*Carrying on cleaning.*) Yes.

Beat. He leaves.

ROSE finishes, is about to go, when she notices someone coming.

Pause.

Thinks.

Decides to go, but before she makes it FLAMM appears.

FLAMM: Rose Bernd!

ROSE stops. Doesn't turn. Pause.

Should offer me a drink at least. Not even worth water these days?

ROSE: Water's there.

FLAMM: I'm not blind. But I don't drink like cattle. Cup in that basket?

ROSE pushes the cover to one side.

A Bunzlauer cup. Well. I like a Bunzlauer cup best of all.

She offers it to him without looking.

If you wouldn't mind.

Beat.

Touch more courtesy?

ROSE goes to the spring, rinses cup, leaves it there and returns to her basket.

No, no, Rose, not like that. That maybe how you get rid of a tramp, I don't know about tramps, I think I'm still the magistrate here, now am I getting a drink or not?

Beat.

One.

Two.

Three. And…

Right, I'm asking politely. No more nonsense.

ROSE goes to the spring, fills the cup, holds it to FLAMM, face averted. He doesn't move.

I can't reach it.

ROSE: You have to hold it!

FLAMM: Can't drink like this.

ROSE: (*Amused against her will, she has to turn to face him.*)
But…

FLAMM: That's better. That's the way.

Steadies the cup, his hand over ROSE's, lowers his mouth to the cup until he has one knee on the floor. Drinks.

You can let go of me now.

ROSE: (*Gently trying to free herself.*) Don't. Let me go, Mr
Flamm…

FLAMM: Think so? Think I should let you go? When I've
got you at last? Don't think I will. Now look at me
properly, look at my face.

I know.

I know about everything

She stops her struggling.

Spoke with Steckel. I know you've agreed.

Beat.

I even know the date of the funeral…sorry, the wedding.

Beat.

It's a tough nut this, Rose. Let's hope we don't crack our
teeth on it.

ROSE: Shouldn't be standing here with you, Mr Flamm.

FLAMM: Don't care about should or shouldn't, if this is
really what's ordained then at least I want to get my
marching orders properly. I won't be shut out.

Beat.

Rose. Did I do something to you that…

That I should apologise for?

ROSE: (*Earnestly.*) Nothing to apologise to me for.

FLAMM: No? Honestly?

ROSE nods.

Good. I'm glad.

Beat.

Was good wasn't it, Rose?

ROSE: Go back to your wife, Mr Flamm.

FLAMM: Good times fly by, what's left?

ROSE: Be good to your wife. Angel, Mr Flamm. Saved me.

FLAMM: Sit with me here, for one minute.

She doesn't.

Always been good to my wife, we're on the best of terms.
Saved? What does that mean? What did she save you
from, what was wrong?

ROSE: Christoph –

Mr Flamm, I can't sit.

Won't get us anywhere. 'S'over now, all taken care of and
God'll forgive the sin. Won't hold it against the chi –

FLAMM: (*Distracted by the growing hum of the threshing
machine.*) That continuous bloody humming! What?
Rose, sit down, I won't do anything, won't touch, I
promise. Tell me. Have faith in me.

ROSE: Don't know…there's…

When I'm married you can ask your wife, maybe she'll
tell you. Haven't told August, but I'm not afraid. He's
good. Kind-hearted, Christian.

Bye Christoph. Goodbye and be healthy. Whole life before us. Now we can be faithful, deny ourselves, work hard, pay our dues and atone.

FLAMM: (*Grasping her hand.*) Wait! Look, Rose, I agree. God knows I'm not coming near your wedding.

Beat.

You first caught my eye as a child. Went through my share of women at the academy, but the first time I felt something was with you.

ROSE: Felt for you as well.

FLAMM: You used to make eyes at me as a little girl.

Pause.

You think about me sometimes? Dirty old Flamm?

ROSE: I will.

FLAMM: Come see us?

ROSE: No.

Just double the pain. Must be an end. Bury myself in the house, work, slave enough for two. The new life, no good looking back at the old one. Earth's just misery and want and we have to get through it to heaven.

FLAMM: So this is it then?

Beat.

ROSE: Father and August'll be wondering –

FLAMM: So it's completely over? Won't even come see the wife?

ROSE: Can't look into her face. Maybe in time, maybe ten years, maybe then it'd be right. Bye, Mr Flamm.

FLAMM: Alright.

    If I weren't –

    Beat.

    Whatever happens, happens. Over.

    He leaves.

ROSE: Whatever happens, happens. Everything's right now.

    She puts the cup back. She packs her stuff away and starts to set off when STRECKMANN appears.

STRECKMANN: Rose?

    Rosie Bernd? Can't you hear me? That Flamm again? Pig, what's he want? Like to get the hands on him, snap some bones. Not on, that, I'm not putting up with this, one man's good as another, I'm not letting him kick me into –

ROSE: What you saying? Who're you?

STRECKMANN: Who'm I? Well you should know.

ROSE: Who are you? Do I know you?

STRECKMANN: Me? D'you know me? Girl, make a monkey out of someone else –

ROSE: What you want? Who are you, what you want with me?

STRECKMANN: Nothing! God's name, don't start scream –

ROSE: Call down the whole world, don't get out of my way!

STRECKMANN: Remember a cherry tree? Remember a crucifix?

ROSE: Who are you? What d'you want from me? Either go or I'll scream!

STRECKMANN: Lost the reason, Girl?

ROSE: Least won't have to drag it round behind me then! Who are you? Liar! You see nothing! I'll scream! Squeeze out every breath in my lungs if you don't go!

STRECKMANN: I'm going, Rose, I'm going; calm down.

ROSE: Now! This minute, understand?

STRECKMANN: Yes, yes, now, why not. Sorry.

Begins to go.

ROSE: Look at it. Worthless filth! When you see it leaving you're seeing the best of it.

She spits. He stops.

Outside it's all spruced up, inside it's being eaten by maggots. Can taste disgust in my throat.

STRECKMANN: (*Turning back.*) What?

Beat.

Don't mean that. What are you saying? Don't sound a very appetising meal. Why were you so hot for it then?

ROSE: Me? Hot for you?

STRECKMANN: Forgotten?

ROSE: Filth!

STRECKMANN: Fair enough.

ROSE: Tramp! Filth! What you sniffing round me for? Who are you? What've I done, you at my heels, hounding, snapping…dog! Butcher's dog!

STRECKMANN: Ran after me back then!

ROSE: What?

STRECKMANN: Came to my door, made me hot as hell.

ROSE: And you?

STRECKMANN: Well, what?

ROSE: You, what about you?

STRECKMANN: I don't refuse what's offered.

ROSE: Streckmann! You'll die one day! Hear? You'll stand before the judge in your last hour! I came to you in God's terror, begged you with the love of the Almighty not to put this thing in the way of me and August, begged on the knees before you, and you say 'ran'? You committed a crime! You committed crime against me, worse than crime, disgusting, Our Lord will savage you for that!

STRECKMANN: Listen to this! I'll take what's coming.

ROSE: You'll take what's coming? Evil! Want to spit in your face!

STRECKMANN: Remember a cherry tree, a crucifix?

ROSE: Swore you wouldn't say that! Swore God's holy oath, laid your hands on the cross and now you're torturing me again! What is it you want?

STRECKMANN: I'm as good as Flamm. I don't want you near him.

ROSE: If I jump into his bed, filth, not anything to do with you.

STRECKMANN: Well. See what happens, then.

ROSE: You committed violence on me! Confused me, wore me down, and swooped like a vulture! I remember! Wanted to get out the door, you ripped my jacket, my dress, there was blood, I was bleeding! Tried to get out, you bolted the door shut. That is crime! Report –

BERND and AUGUST enter, followed by KLEINART, GOLISCH and the workers.

BERND: What's this? What've you done to my child?

AUGUST: (*Pulling BERND back and pushing himself forward.*) Father, I'll deal with…What did you do to Rosie?

STRECKMANN: Nothing.

AUGUST: (*In STRECKMANN's face.*) What're you doing to this girl?

STRECKMANN: Nothing!

AUGUST: Tell us what you were doing!

STRECKMANN: Nothing! Strike me dead if I touched her!

AUGUST: Say what you did…or –

STRECKMANN: 'Or'? Or what? Or what, then?

AUGUST grabs STRECKMANN.

KLEINART: Stop this!

STRECKMANN: Off my throat!

BERND: Believe us, either –

STRECKMANN: Help!

They have pulled AUGUST away.

AUGUST: What did you do? Answer! Answer me! I want to know!

AUGUST frees himself and goes for STRECKMANN, who suddenly lashes out with his fist catching AUGUST in the eye.

STRECKMANN: There! That's what I did!

KLEINART: Streckma –

MRS GOLISCH: Catch August, he's falling!

HEAD MAID: (*Holding AUGUST.*) August?

BERND: (*Ignoring AUGUST, straight to STRECKMANN.*) Account for this! This'll be at your door!

STRECKMANN: Pig shit! Because of a woman who'll fuck with anyone!

He leaves.

BERND: What did he say?

KLEINART, GOLISCH, HEAD MAID and MRS GOLISCH are holding AUGUST up.

KLEINART: His eye's out!

MRS GOLISCH: Father Bernd? August is hurt.

KLEINART: He's had a cursed engagement.

BERND: What's happened? Holy God in Heaven! August?

AUGUST: My eye hurts.

BERND: Rose, bring water.

MRS GOLISCH: Is misfortune…

BERND: Rose, bring water! Didn't you hear?

GOLISCH: Cost him a year in prison, this.

ROSE: (*As if coming to.*) He says…he's saying…Yes. What does that mean? I hear…got a doll for Christmas…

HEAD MAID: Are you sleeping, girl?

ROSE: Nobody can tell. No, Head maid. 'S'not right. Shouldn't be done. Should perhaps…girl needs a mother.

Four

FLAMM's house, Saturday afternoon, early September. FLAMM at his desk doing accounts. STRECKMANN standing in front of him.

Silence.

FLAMM: Two hundred and six…and thirty.

STRECKMANN: Yes, Mr Flamm.

FLAMM: Something wrong with the machine?

STRECKMANN looks blank.

You took a morning off.

STRECKMANN: Nothing wrong with machine. Appeared in district court.

Beat.

FLAMM: Was it to do with Keil?

STRECKMANN: Yes.

Beat.

That and Bernd suing me for slandering his girl.

FLAMM: (*Counting out the money.*) Two hundred…two hundred and six…and fifty… You owe me twenty.

STRECKMANN takes the money. Counts. Puts it in his pocket and puts some coins on the table, which FLAMM puts away without even looking. Pause.

STRECKMANN: Should I tell the high bailiff you'll want me again, mid-December?

FLAMM: Beginning of December. Two days. Empty the big barn.

STRECKMANN: Beginning December. Yes, sir. Goodbye.

FLAMM: Bye.

STRECKMANN is almost out.

What'll be the outcome?

STRECKMANN stops.

Of all that?

Beat.

STRECKMANN: Not much of an outcome for me, Mr Flamm.

FLAMM: Oh?

STRECKMANN: Will have to suffer.

FLAMM: Why were you fighting?

STRECKMANN: Can't remember. Must've been out of it. Truth is, can't remember nothing.

FLAMM: Heard that bookbinder is…placid.

STRECKMANN: Always starting rows with me!

Beat.

Like it's been ripped out my memory. Just know they fell on me like wolves, otherwise accident wouldn't've happened.

FLAMM: The eye couldn't be saved?

STRECKMANN: No.

Which I'm sorry for.

FLAMM: Bad enough in itself, but when the courts get involved, things only go to bad.

The girl I feel sorry for.

STRECKMANN: Lost weight, that's how it affected me. Don't know what sleep is anymore, Mr Flamm. Don't have anything against August, I just…can't remember.

FLAMM: Should go see Bernd. If you slandered the girl but were worse for wear, you could just make a retraction.

STRECKMANN: Not my business. His. If he knew what'll come out he'd take back his accusations.

Someone should tell him. That he's not helping the girl, that is. Bye, Your Honour.

FLAMM: Streckmann.

STRECKMANN leaves.

Only I could put my fingers round your neck.

MRS FLAMM enters, pushed in by the MAID.

MRS FLAMM: What are you muttering, Flamm?

She signals the MAID to leave.

Trouble with someone?

FLAMM: Yes, thank you, it's fine.

MRS FLAMM: Was that Streckmann?

FLAMM: The lovely Streckmann, yes, that was the lovely Streckmann.

Beat.

MRS FLAMM: Did you talk about Keil?

FLAMM: (*Scribbling.*) What? Look, my head is full of these figures…

MRS FLAMM: Am I disturbing you, Christel?

FLAMM: No, but you must be quiet.

MRS FLAMM: The one thing I can guarantee you.

Silence.

FLAMM: Jesus Christ! Sometimes I just want to shoot scum like that! Be a joke, having that on my conscience.

MRS FLAMM: Christel, you're frightening me.

FLAMM: That man is so disgusting, worse than any criminal I've… At least sometimes, but… I mean I'm no saint, but he makes the bowels twist in my body.

MRS FLAMM: What's made you so angry?

FLAMM: (*Writing.*) I'm just…talking in general terms.

MRS FLAMM: Oh.

Beat.

Only I thought you were talking about Streckmann

Pause. He carries on with his work.

Christel, I can't get this business out of my mind. And maybe when you have a minute we could talk about –

FLAMM: What's Streckmann got to do with me?

MRS FLAMM: Maybe not Streckmann himself, but Old Bernd and Rose Bernd. If I hadn't been stuck here I would've liked to have gone to see her. She never comes here, so –

FLAMM: What for?

MRS FLAMM: I need to see that she's alright.

Beat.

FLAMM: Fine, fine, do what you feel you have to. You'll have a job on your hands, though.

MRS FLAMM: What does that mean?

FLAMM: Shouldn't get involved in other people's business. Get nothing but trouble, ingratitude.

MRS FLAMM: So? We can bear a little trouble and ingratitude is the way of the world. And Rose… It's like she was our own child.

Beat.

I remember her standing in the churchyard by Kurt's grave. I was closer then to death than life, but I can see it still. She felt almost as much pain as we did.

FLAMM: Fine. So what're you going to do? I don't know what you're going to do!

Beat.

MRS FLAMM: I want to ask you about something.

FLAMM: About what?

MRS FLAMM: Look, you know I don't usually interfere, but now… I want to know what's been the matter with you recently?

FLAMM: With me? I thought you were talking about Rose Bernd?

MRS FLAMM: Well now I'm talking about you.

FLAMM: Well you can stop wasting your breath, wife, because my affairs are none of your business.

MRS FLAMM: That's easy to say. But when you have to sit – as I am forced to sit – and watch how disturbed someone is and know that he's not sleeping, listen to him sighing and if that person happens to be your husband you become concerned.

FLAMM: Are you trying to make me sound stupid? Sighing? Whatever else, I'm not some nancy-boy.

MRS FLAMM: Christel, you don't get away from me like that.

FLAMM: Are you being deliberately irritating? Are you trying to bore me, drive me out of the house? Is that what you want? Because you're doing a great job of it.

MRS FLAMM: You're hiding something.

Beat. He shrugs.

FLAMM: Maybe. Think what you like. All got problems. Yesterday I had to sack a brewers man; day before I sent a distiller to Satan. And this life here is enough to drive any decent man insane.

MRS FLAMM: If you need company, go into town.

FLAMM: Oh yes, playing skat with the regulars at the Horse? Have what passes for a conversation with the Prefect? God help me! Weren't for hunting, if I couldn't shoulder my gun occasionally, I'd run off to sea.

MRS FLAMM: You see? That's what I'm talking about. You've changed completely. Two, three months ago you were content; occupied yourself hunting, botany, you sang, Christel. But you've changed.

FLAMM: If only Kurt had stayed with us.

Pause.

MRS FLAMM: What...

if we adopted a child?

FLAMM: Now? Now? I don't want to now. You couldn't make up your mind then, well, now the moment has passed.

MRS FLAMM: It's easy to say 'let's get a child'! It seemed like betrayal, even considering it seemed like a betrayal.

Like we were shoving Kurt away from us, out of the house, out of our hearts, Flamm. And where would we find a child that could bring us hope? Where –

Beat.

Leave that where it is. Get back to Rose. Flamm, do you know what's wrong with her?

FLAMM: I… Yes, I, of course. Why wouldn't I? Streckmann has slandered her conduct, Old Bernd won't tolerate it. Stupid to sue. Woman suffers in the end.

MRS FLAMM: I wrote to Rose asking her to come here, in her situation she won't know what to do.

FLAMM: And why's that?

MRS FLAMM: Because Streckmann is right.

Beat.

FLAMM: Say what you mean!

MRS FLAMM: Christel, there is no need to be angry straight away! I haven't spoken to you about this because I know how you are about these things. You threw the Under-Maid out of the house, remember the beating you gave the bag-maker? She confessed to me, nearly eight weeks ago, that she's no longer just Rose Bernd. A second being has to be taken into consideration. One that's on the way.

Flamm? Did you hear what I said?

FLAMM: What?

No. Yes, I, not completely, I…

Beat.

I feel a bit dizzy. Sometimes I get…

I need some air. Don't worry, it's not… Don't worry, wife.

MRS FLAMM: What are you doing with that cartridge pouch?

FLAMM: Nothing? What am I doing with this cartridge pouch?

Puts it down.

Told nothing. Sometimes I feel like a complete stranger in this world.

MRS FLAMM: Christel, what does that mean?

FLAMM: Nothing. Nothing at all, just nothing. I'm fine now. I just sometimes get this feeling like I'm…falling.

MRS FLAMM: You're very odd today.

There is a knock.

Who's that now? Come in!

AUGUST: (*Outside.*) Just me, Mrs Flamm.

Beat. FLAMM leaves, into the hunting room.

MRS FLAMM: Oh.

It's you, Mr Keil. Well, come in.

AUGUST enters, dark glasses, eye patch.

AUGUST: Come with apologies, Mrs Flamm. Good morning, Mrs Flamm.

MRS FLAMM: Keil.

AUGUST: My fiancé has appointment at the district court, Mrs Flamm, which is why she cannot come.

Beat.

Maybe this evening.

MRS FLAMM: Nice to have the chance to see you.

Pause.

Sit down. How are you?

AUGUST: Lord's ways are mysterious. When he strikes us, we mustn't complain. Should rejoice.

And that's how it is with me, Mrs Flamm, almost.

Fine.

Worse things get, happier I am; treasury in the afterlife is increasing.

MRS FLAMM: I hope you're right, Mr Keil. Did Rose get my letters?

AUGUST: Read them to her. And I said, definitely, that this wasn't on, that she must come and visit you straight away.

MRS FLAMM: Well, I'm surprised, Keil, that after everything that's happened she hasn't found her way here. She knows she'll find a sympathetic ear.

AUGUST: She's become shy. And, Mrs Flamm, if you don't mind, you shouldn't take offence. Lot on her plate. Caring for me. Then, since that man's slanders, doesn't like to come out the room.

MRS FLAMM: I don't take offence, Keil. And how is she otherwise?

AUGUST: What can I say? Had to be in court eleven o'clock today – led us the dance. It's just…

It's frightening how she's talking; first she won't go, then she'll go but with me, then she bolts like lightning, shouting at me not to follow.

Sometimes she weeps.

Beat.

Makes you think.

MRS FLAMM: Think what?

AUGUST: Things.

This thing that happened to me, keeps talking about it.
Cut her soul, how it's affecting Father Bernd, how he's
taken it to heart –

MRS FLAMM: We are alone here, Mr Keil. Let's speak
openly. Have you ever thought…This business with
Streckmann, has it occurred to you or perhaps to Father
Bernd that there might be some truth in it?

Beat.

AUGUST: Don't let myself think.

MRS FLAMM: Alright. Can't blame you for that.
Sometimes the only thing we can do is…

But this attitude is not right for a Father.

Beat.

AUGUST: Mrs Flamm, he's far from thinking something
might be wrong. Hard as stone, have the hands cut off
him first, you wouldn't believe the strictness in this. Even
when His Honour was there, trying to persuade him to
withdraw the charge –

MRS FLAMM: Who was there?

AUGUST: His Honour. Mr Flamm

MRS FLAMM: My husband?

AUGUST: Yes. Talked long. I've lost an eye, but I don't
care whether Streckmann is punished. Vengeance is

mine, saith the Lord. Father is not so quick to forgive.
Ask anything but that, he –

MRS FLAMM: My husband was with Old Bernd?

AUGUST: Yes, when he got the summons.

MRS FLAMM: What summons was this?

AUGUST: Appear before the examining magistrate.

MRS FLAMM: Old Bernd?

AUGUST: Mr Flamm.

Beat.

MRS FLAMM: My husband was examined as well? What
does he have to do with the case?

Beat.

AUGUST: He was examined as well.

Yes.

MRS FLAMM: Really? That's…

news.

I didn't know that. Or that Christel went to see Old
Bernd, I…

Pause.

Go home, August. Please, I'm a little…unsure.

If you really love the girl…

Beat.

Look at me: let me tell you something. When someone's
made that way – whether it's a man that women run after
or a woman that men want, our lot is to suffer. Suffer. Be

patient. Lived this way for twelve years, looking at things through the cracks in my fingers.

AUGUST: Can't believe that –

MRS FLAMM: Believe it or don't, life doesn't ask what you believe.

I said I'd look after Rose: easy to make a promise, hard to keep one. I'll do whatever is in my power.

Goodbye. I don't expect you to…

Beat.

God owes us his pity.

She shakes his hand. AUGUST leaves.

MRS FLAMM sits thinking. After a moment FLAMM enters, quiet. Looks at his wife. She doesn't return the look.

Pause.

He starts whistling quietly, pretends to be looking for something.

That's right; whistle. But I didn't think even you were capable of this.

FLAMM turns to her, considers, then shrugs weakly.

You men, these things are nothing. Well, what's going to happen now?

FLAMM: (*Shrugs again.*) Not sure. Let's keep calm. Tell you about what happened, maybe you'll judge me less.

MRS FLAMM: Such recklessness can't be judged mildly.

FLAMM: Recklessness? Wasn't recklessness. Which would be better, wife, recklessness or something deeper – ?

MRS FLAMM: Destroying the future of this girl? This girl who I…for who we have a responsibility? We lured her into this house, blind faith in us. I want the earth to devour us. It's as if we planned it.

FLAMM: Have you finished?

MRS FLAMM: No I haven't!

FLAMM: I'll wait.

MRS FLAMM: Christel, what did I say to you when you asked me to marry you?

FLAMM: I don't know.

MRS FLAMM: I'm too old for you. A wife can be sixteen years younger in this world but not three or four older. Why didn't you listen to me?

FLAMM: What's the point in raking over the past? I had no idea what she meant to me until now. Of course I'd've acted differently, but now we have to see what we can salvage, which is why I wanted to ask you not to be petty, I wanted to see whether you could –

Everything was honourable until suddenly Rose was to marry that twitching idiot. Once it was decided, I lost control of… I'm becoming confused.

I watched that little girl grow up and some of our love for Kurt clung to her. I only thought of protecting her, saving her from the misfortune. At first. Then suddenly…

It's like Plato says in Phaedrus when he talks about two horses; the bad horse got the better of me and the dam broke.

Silence.

MRS FLAMM: What a lovely story. Even threw in the odd learned reference. And so you think you are right. The poor women just have to manage, because you did it to protect Rose, sacrificing yourself in the process. There aren't excuses for this, Flamm.

FLAMM: Fine, forget it. But remember when Kurt died I couldn't stand to have that girl in the house! Who was it enticed her in here?

MRS FLAMM: So that not everything in this house would be dead!

FLAMM: I said nothing for your sake.

MRS FLAMM: Every tear shed for your sort is a waste of salt!

HEAD MAID brings in coffee.

HEAD MAID: Rose Bernd's in the kitchen.

MRS FLAMM: Come, girl. Push me out.

(*To FLAMM.*) Help push me out of the way; there must be some space you can tuck me into where I won't be an obstruction. When I've gone call her in.

FLAMM: (*To HEAD MAID.*) Tell her to wait.

HEAD MAID goes out.

Speak to her. I can't. My hands are tied.

Beat.

MRS FLAMM: And what should I say?

FLAMM: You know that better than me. You know what… You said it yourself, you… Just don't be cruel, for God's sake! She mustn't leave here like this.

MRS FLAMM: I can't clean her boots, Flamm!

FLAMM: I'm not asking you to! But you asked her to come, you can't just drop all your compassion and sympathy – what did you say to me? It's the girl that suffers. And if this girl suffers like that…I'm not so depraved that I'll just carry on –

Beat.

It's in your hands. Don't forget that.

Pause.

MRS FLAMM: Christel, you're not worth it.

But when it comes to it, what am I supposed to do?

Alright. Fine. I'll talk to her. But please don't imagine that I can mend what you've smashed and shattered. You men are like children.

The HEAD MAID re-enters.

HEAD MAID: Won't wait no more.

MRS FLAMM: Send her in.

HEAD MAID leaves.

FLAMM: Be clever, wife, or on my word of honour –

MRS FLAMM: Don't give it then you won't have to break it.

FLAMM leaves. MRS FLAMM waits.

ROSE enters, Sunday best, though she looks pale.

ROSE: 'Day Madam.

MRS FLAMM: Good day, Rose. Sit down. Well. I asked you to come…

Beat. MRS FLAMM gathers herself.

You remember what was said when we spoke before. Well things have changed. Today I understand more why you didn't want my help. But I cannot see how you'll get through this on your own.

Beat.

Come and drink coffee with me.

ROSE sits near the table.

August's been here. If I had been in your shoes child, I'd've risked the truth with him long ago.

Beat.

Older I get, the less I understand this world. We all get our piece of life the same way, from Emperor to Archbishop to stable boy, but no-one's allowed to talk about it.

ROSE: Madam, everything'd be peace if it weren't for Streckmann. He's a liar and a –

MRS FLAMM: Girl, how can you say he's lying? It can almost be seen on you.

Beat.

ROSE: He's lying, that's all I know.

He's…lying.

MRS FLAMM: But in what respect is he lying?

ROSE: Every respect, every way.

MRS FLAMM: You don't seem to be thinking. Who is it sits in front of you?

No answer.

You confessed to me! And now I know more, Rose, I know it all.

ROSE: You were killing me, couldn't say I knew more.

Beat.

MRS FLAMM: So this is your game now? Would've judged you different, I didn't expect this. I hope you spoke less gibberish in court.

ROSE: Said same in court.

MRS FLAMM stares at her.

MRS FLAMM: Girl, come to your senses! You can't lie like that before a judge! Listen to me!

Look, take a mouthful of coffee and don't be frightened. No-one's after you. You haven't been good to me, Rose, not by any reckoning. If you'd told me the truth back then, maybe we'd've found a way out, but now –

Right. The main thing – and you can rely on this – is that you won't suffer want. Either of you. If Bernd throws you out, if August leaves you, provision will be made for you and your child.

ROSE: Don't…know what you mean, Madam.

MRS FLAMM: What? Well, if you've forgotten that, then maybe you've got a bad conscience. Then maybe you're guilty of other things. And maybe those things are to do with Streckmann; he's the one bringing this trouble on you.

ROSE: How can you say that? For the sake of God, how've I deserved this?

MRS FLAMM: You have changed… I can't believe how much you've changed.

ROSE: Should've died with my mother. Said she'd take me –

MRS FLAMM: Come to your senses, girl, you're alive! What's wrong?

ROSE: Had nothing with Streckmann! That man has lied the blue out of the sky.

MRS FLAMM: What lies? Did he lie under oath?

Beat.

ROSE: Under oath or not, same.

MRS FLAMM: Were you under oath?

ROSE: Don't know… I'm not a bad person, if I'd done that it'd be bad. I wasn't… August lost his eye, I wasn't… Have to work, pray and save something from the flames of this world or they break your strength –

FLAMM enters.

FLAMM: Who's breaking your strength? Look at her, we're trying to save you.

ROSE: Too late.

FLAMM: What's that mean?

ROSE: Nothing. Can't wait longer. Goodbye.

FLAMM: Stay there! Don't you move! I heard everything at the door and now I want the truth –

ROSE: Told truth.

FLAMM: About Streckmann.

Pause.

ROSE: Nothing. He's lying.

FLAMM: Does he say there's something? Between you?

ROSE: Saying nothing except he's lying!

FLAMM: Did he swear that lie in court?

Pause. She cannot answer. FLAMM stares at her.

Well, wife, I'm sorry, forgive what you can. As for this…nothing to do with me anymore. I'm disgusted with it.

MRS FLAMM: (*To ROSE.*) Did you deny everything?

ROSE: …

FLAMM: I spoke the truth in court. And Streckmann doesn't lie at such moments. Perjury gets you prison, you don't lie.

MRS FLAMM: Girl, did you not speak truth? Did you lie under oath? Do you know what you've started? When did you come to be so stupid?

ROSE: Was ashamed!

MRS FLAMM: But Rose –

FLAMM: Don't waste your breath. Why did you lie to a judge?

ROSE: Ashamed, I was…

FLAMM: And me? The wife? August? Why cheat us? And probably Streckmann too and whoever else you were carrying on with. Looks so honest, but you're right to be ashamed.

ROSE: He hunted me like a dog!

FLAMM: Women make dogs of men. One man today, tomorrow another… Do what you want now. Whatever you like. If I raise one finger to help you I swear I'll find a rope and beat myself blind with it.

ROSE stares at FLAMM.

MRS FLAMM: What I've said stands; provision will be made.

ROSE: I was…

Beat.

I was ashamed.

MRS FLAMM: Listening, Rose?

ROSE leaves.

Rose?

Pause.

Girl's gone.

Beat.

FLAMM: (*Shaken.*) Henrietta?

God forgive me.

Five

BERND's house, clean but cold, full of religious imagery. Evening, the same day.

Voices outside.

KLEINART: (*Outside.*) Bernd? Home?

> We'll go round back.

He enters with ROSE. She looks exhausted, leaning on him.

ROSE: All dark.

> *Beat.*

KLEINART: Not leaving you like this.

ROSE: Nothing wrong with me

KLEINART: Tell it to someone else, girl. Wouldn't't've had to pick you up off the ground there was nothing wrong with you.

ROSE: Got bit dizzy. Honest, better now, don't need help now…

KLEINART: Not leaving you like this.

ROSE: …in good condition again. This happens sometimes, it's nothing –

KLEINART: Lying half dead by that willow! Writhing like a worm under the tree.

ROSE: Kleinart, go… Have to light the fire. Be here soon for their meal.

> *Beat.*

> Tired.

KLEINART: And you're lighting fires? Shouldn't do that, should be in bed.

ROSE: Kleinart, go home.

Beat.

I don't want Father or August knowing.

She fetches a candle.

Look; well again.

KLEINART: Just saying that.

ROSE: Because it's true.

MARTHEL enters, apron bulging with potatoes.

Here's Marthel as well.

MARTHEL: Rose? Where you been all day?

ROSE: Dreamed I was in court.

KLEINART: You were in court!

Look after the sister, Marthla, least till Father gets back, she's not herself.

ROSE: Get fire going, Marthla. Where's Father?

MARTHEL: On August's land.

ROSE: And August?

MARTHEL: Don't know. Not in the fields today.

ROSE: Have you got new potatoes?

Beat. MARTHEL empties her apron, which is full of potatoes, onto the floor.

Oh.

ROSE goes to make a move but can't because of pain.

Fetch the bowl and pan, Martha.

KLEINART: Shall I send for someone?

ROSE: Grave-digger.

She peels. They watch.

KLEINART: Well, goodbye.

ROSE: (*Still not looking up.*) Goodbye.

MARTHEL: Come again, Godfather Kleinart.

KLEINART leaves.

You not well?

ROSE: I'm well.

But she is muttering to herself, perhaps a prayer.

MARTHEL: Rose?

ROSE: What?

MARTHEL: What's the matter?

ROSE: Bring the pan and some potatoes.

MARTHEL does so.

MARTHEL: I'm scared. Way you look…

ROSE: Is it on my hands?

Beat.

Things seem strange to me.

Weak laugh.

Jesus. Can't look at the face. Hands. Eyes.

MARTHEL: Rosla, has something happened?

ROSE: God protect you from what's happened, wish yourself dead first: they say if you die early she's at peace, you don't need to live and draw breath. What happened to little Kurt Flamm? don't remember. Bit dizzy. Forgotten, forgetting things, life is hard, if only I could stay forgetting.

MARTHEL: Wish Father were here…

ROSE: Don't say anything to the Father, that I was here, Marthel. You promise? Done so many things for you, Marthla, don't forget that, even in this dark.

MARTHEL: D'you want coffee? There's a drop left. I'm frightened, Rosla.

ROSE: Don't be frightened.

Beat.

I'll just go to the bed for a bit, just lie down for a bit. I'm alright, nothing wrong.

MARTHEL: What should I say?

ROSE: Not one word.

MARTHEL: And nothing to August?

ROSE: Not a syllable. Betray me now and it's dead between us.

Beat.

MARTHEL: Rosla, not something bad, is it? I mean nothing harmful?

ROSE: Don't think so. Come here, Marthla.

MARTHEL supports ROSE.

Too often alone in this world. Too often lonely. Only we weren't so lonely.

They leave.

The house is empty for a moment.

BERND appears, hoe in hand.

MARTHEL re-enters.

MARTHEL: Father?

BERND: No hot water? Want my footbath. Rose not here?

MARTHEL: Not here, no.

BERND: What? Not back from court? Nearly eight. August here?

MARTHEL: Not yet.

BERND: Not yet either? Perhaps she's with August.

Did you see that cloud, Marthel? About six? Coming in from the Peaks?

MARTHEL: Went all dark.

BERND: Day's coming that'll be darker than that. Light the lamp and set out the Holy Scripture. Marthel, do you think constantly of your death so you'll be able to stand before the judge eternal?

Beat. She nods.

Few do.

Beat.

Someone shouting at me again: 'Slave-driver'.

Wasn't a slave-driver; did my duty. Powers of darkness are strong! Back-scratching, shutting both eyes, ignoring the cheating, then you're popular with people, well I lean on Jesus, not people. Just doing good isn't enough.

Maybe your sister'd kept this in mind…

CONSTABLE appears.

Who's that?

CONSTABLE: I have a summons to serve.

No-one moves.

Like to speak with your girl.

BERND: My eldest?

CONSTABLE: (*Reading.*) 'Rose Bernd'.

BERND: She's not back from court. Can I give it to her?

CONSTABLE: No.

Need make...

personal investigation.

Awkward pause.

Well then: back tomorrow at eight.

AUGUST enters.

BERND: August?

AUGUST: Is Rose here?

BERND: This constable's asking after her. Thought you'd be with her.

CONSTABLE: I have questions to ask and this to serve.

AUGUST: Always this Streckmann business.

Beat.

CONSTABLE: Good evening. Tomorrow at eight.

He leaves.

AUGUST: Marthel, go in the kitchen. Father, I want to talk
–

Go, Marthel, go and close the door. Marthel, have you seen Rose?

MARTHEL: No.

Beckoning him.

Can I tell you something, August?

AUGUST: No time, girl, shut the door.

She shuts the door.

Father, you must withdraw this action.

Beat.

BERND: What?

AUGUST: It's not Christian. You must withdraw.

BERND: 'Not…'?

Why?

AUGUST: How do I say this? Father Bernd…you have been too hot in this affair.

Beat.

BERND: Too hot? How have I been too hot? What about the child's honour? The honour of my house, of my wife in her grave. You, August, what about your honour?

AUGUST: How do I start, Father Bernd, when you are so unforgiving?

We should not seek our own honour, but the honour of God and no other.

BERND: Here the woman's honour and God's honour is the same!

Beat.

Are you making complaint against Rose?

AUGUST: I've told you, I have no complaint.

BERND: Have you something you feel guilty of regarding her?

AUGUST: I would never deviate in the slightest way from –

BERND: Well, then.

Beat.

I know. I know that of you, August. Let justice take the course.

AUGUST: Only we knew where she was.

BERND: Maybe she's not back from the court.

AUGUST: Don't take that long, said she'd be home by five.

BERND: Maybe she's buying. Don't you have things to buy?

AUGUST: She has no money with her, and what we needed for the shop we were getting together.

BERND: Thought she'd be with you.

AUGUST: Went more than a mile to meet her. No sign.

Met Streckmann instead.

BERND: Then you met Satan.

AUGUST: Father, he has a wife and a child. Why should they suffer his sins? What do I get from him in prison? If there's repentance…I don't want more –

BERND: That thing and repentance?

AUGUST: Seemed like he did.

BERND: You spoke with him?

Beat.

AUGUST: Wouldn't let me go. Ran next to me talking, no-one else for miles, just us on the road. I felt sorry for him, couldn't help but.

BERND: So what did it say?

AUGUST: Said you should withdraw.

BERND: How could I look you in the face if I let that stick to her, now, after what we've been through?

They've always been snapping at our heels, August, because we live different. Creeps and hypocrites, they call us. Slave-drivers. Always wanted something to control us with, well what a feast this'd be for them. Girl has been reared like this, God-fearing and hardworking, so that when I hand her to a Christian man she can bring up a Christian house. This is how it is! And this is how I'll hand her over. Should I let this poison stick to her? Rather live on salt and potatoes for the rest of my life, than take a penny of your money.

AUGUST: Father Bernd, God's ways are mysterious, sends us new tests every day – we must never rest self-righteous. And if we wanted to we couldn't.

Father, I cannot spare you this; our Rose has been human.

Beat.

BERND: What does that mean?

AUGUST: Don't ask more, Father.

Pause. BERND sits.

Places his hand on the Bible. Leafs through.

Stops. Looks at AUGUST.

BERND: I don't understand.

Have I been blind...?

Beat.

August, don't let Streckmann have you. He's trapped;
judgement's coming home to him and he wants to sneak
out any means he can, set you against the girl. Can't we
see through this filth? Hunted this girl, doesn't snare her
one way tries another and now it's trying this. Trying to
split you up! Happened before, good people split by
Satan and his intrigues, people who the Lord had created
for each other. They resent you this girl!

Beat.

Well, alright. I'm not throwing Rose at you. We can have
enough as well! But if you'll listen to one word...I would
put my right hand into fire before –

AUGUST: Mr Flamm swore an oath.

BERND: And?

AUGUST: Father Bernd –

BERND: Wait a minute, August...

Gets books ledgers, hat, collection box.

Oaths? I'll swear oaths. My hat of office, collection box
for the missions. I'm putting them here, so that if there's
a shred of truth in what you say I'll take these to the
pastor and no-one'll see me here again.

So.

Go on. Say what you have to say.

AUGUST: I had the same thoughts.

Perhaps sell the house and land.

Beat.

Maybe we could find peace elsewhere.

BERND: (*Shocked.*) Sell the house and land?

Pause. Father BERND crosses himself. AUGUST is shocked.

How does it come to this? Is it judgement day? This the last hour, how did it get to this, August?

AUGUST: Father Bernd, I don't intend to leave her.

BERND: Do as you like. No concern of mine what kind of person other men allow in their houses. But I'm not that sort of man.

Well then.

AUGUST: Can say only this; something must've happened. Whether with Flamm or Streckmann –

BERND: Two?

AUGUST: I don't know.

BERND: Feel like there's disease clinging to the body.

MARTHEL bursts in, breathless.

MARTHEL: Think Rose had accident! She's upstairs. Been home this time.

AUGUST: Rose?

MARTHEL: Think she's coming down.

BERND: God forgive, I cannot look at it.

He sits, hands over his ears staring into the Scripture.

ROSE Appears. She is struggling to stay upright, her pigtails loosened. She scans the room. AUGUST turns away.

Silence.

ROSE: Cheers everyone!

Pause.

AUGUST: Same.

Beat.

ROSE: Don't want me here I'll go.

AUGUST: Where'll you go? And where've you been?

ROSE: Ask questions, you'll hear answers. More than you'd like. Marthel, come here.

MARTHEL goes to her.

(*Loudly.*) What's wrong with Father?

MARTHEL: Don't know.

ROSE: (*To BERND.*) What's matter with you, then? Speak up!

And you August; what's the matter with you? You've reason to despise me, I don't contest that.

AUGUST: I don't despise anyone –

ROSE: Well, I do. All the lot of you.

AUGUST: Dark, what you're saying.

ROSE: It's dark. Yes. I agree. World's dark. You can hear the roaring of savage beasts in it, and then one day it gets lighter…but it's just the flames of hell that's illuminating things. Marthla –

BERND: (*Grabbing MARTHEL from ROSE.*) Don't poison my child! Leave her! Go to your room.

MARTHEL leaves, tears.

I wish I couldn't see. Wish I couldn't hear. Wish I was a corpse.

Buries himself back into his bible.

ROSE: I'm alive! I'm standing here. This is something, that I'm standing here, Father, thought even you could understand that! Nothing more you can do to me. Oh, Jesus, you live in this tiny little room, you've no idea there's a world out there. I know. I've learned in spasms of agony. Everything falls away, one wall after another and suddenly you're outside in this…storm, and there's nothing above or below you. You're all children compared to this.

AUGUST: Rose, if it's true, what Streckmann says, then you might have sworn a false oath and –

ROSE: Don't know.

Could be.

Can't remember right now. World is made of lies and deceptions.

BERND: God be my refuge…

AUGUST: This how you take the swearing of false oaths?

ROSE: That's nothing. That's nothing at all. What would that be when there's something on the ground. Now that's something. That thing lying by the willow. That is something. Rest don't bother me.

I lay there and looked up into the stars. I screamed and I called out and I saw no sign of a Heavenly Father stirring to help me.

BERND: You're blaspheming our Heavenly Father? I don't know you.

ROSE: You do know me, Father. You cradled me on your knees and I stood by you. Something's overshadowing us all – I fought and I fought –

BERND: What is it?

ROSE: Don't know. Don't know what it is.

Sits on the floor.

AUGUST: Rosla, stand up. I'm not abandoning you. Stand up! All sinners, every one of us, but if you repent you will be forgiven. Stand, Rose! Father, lift her. We're not here to condemn you, at least I'm not. Whatever happens I'm staying with you, I'm not a judge, I don't judge. Our Saviour didn't judge. He bore sickness for us and we watched as he was tortured by God. Maybe we've all made mistakes, I've thought about this and I don't let myself off. Before she even got to know me she had to say yes and amen. What do I care what they think?

ROSE: August, you hung about my neck like chains. Couldn't walk down the road, men, at me.

BERND: Listen to it! You used to boast you'd like to see a man try to get the better of you – you hit the miller's boy in the face! Girl who does that, you said, deserves no pity, should hang herself! Now it talks of traps.

ROSE: Because now I know.

AUGUST: Rose, I'm going to stay by you. Sell the land. We could travel. I've an uncle in Brazil. We'll grab our piece of living somehow, one way or another. Maybe it's only now we're ripe for each other.

ROSE: Jesus, Jesus, what have I done? Crept home? Why didn't I stay with my baby?

Beat.

AUGUST: With what?

ROSE: Finished, August. First it burnt like fire in my belly, then I was dizzy.

BERND: D'you understand this?

AUGUST: No, nothing.

BERND: Know what I feel? Like one abyss after the other keeps opening up in front of me, again and again. What do I have to hear to next?

ROSE: Curse; meet you at judgement, tear the throat out through your jaw.

AUGUST: Who do you mean, Rose?

ROSE: Who it is, knows.

She sinks into a chair.

Silence.

AUGUST: What is this that's on you?

ROSE: Don't know. Asked me earlier, perhaps... Now, don't know. Not loved enough.

AUGUST: Don't know which is more violent; happy love or unhappy love.

ROSE: Was strong. Not now. Over.

CONSTABLE enters.

They stare at him. ROSE giggles

CONSTABLE: Old Kleinart says she's already home.

AUGUST: We didn't...we didn't know before –

CONSTABLE: Rather get it over with now. There's something to sign.

Puts papers on the table.

AUGUST: Rose? Something here.

ROSE is laughing.

CONSTABLE: You'll find nothing to laugh at here, girl. If you don't mind...

ROSE: Can you...wait

a moment.

AUGUST: Why?

ROSE: Not well.

Killed the child.

Beat.

AUGUST: What are you saying? What's she saying?

CONSTABLE: Something to do with this Streckmann –

ROSE: Streckmann? He killed my child.

BERND: Quiet, girl, the mind's gone.

CONSTABLE: You have no child –

ROSE: What did these hands kill, then?

I killed my child with these hands.

CONSTABLE: You possessed? What's wrong with you?

ROSE: I'm completely clear.

Not possessed. Woke up with a clear mind. Wasn't to live. Shouldn't. Didn't want it to. Didn't want it feeling torments. Was to stay where it belonged.

AUGUST: Rose, stop torturing yourself, us. Don't know what you're doing, making us all miserable –

Rose has brought her hand out from under her skirt. It has blood on it. Beat.

ROSE: You know nothing, See nothing, eyes open but completely blind.

Go look behind the willow.

They stare at her.

Go on then.

By the alder-trees. Parson's field…by that pool. There's something small on the ground.

BERND: Done something like this?

AUGUST: Rose? Done something like this?

She is now in no state to answer.

CONSTABLE: Needs to come with me, now. Make confession. It'll help.

AUGUST: Rose?

CONSTABLE: Think it'll help.

End.